U.S. Fish & Wildlife Service

Sea Ducks in the Atlantic Flyway: Population Status and a Review of Special Hunting Seasons

David F. Caithamer

Mark Otto

Paul I. Padding

John R. Sauer

George H. Haas

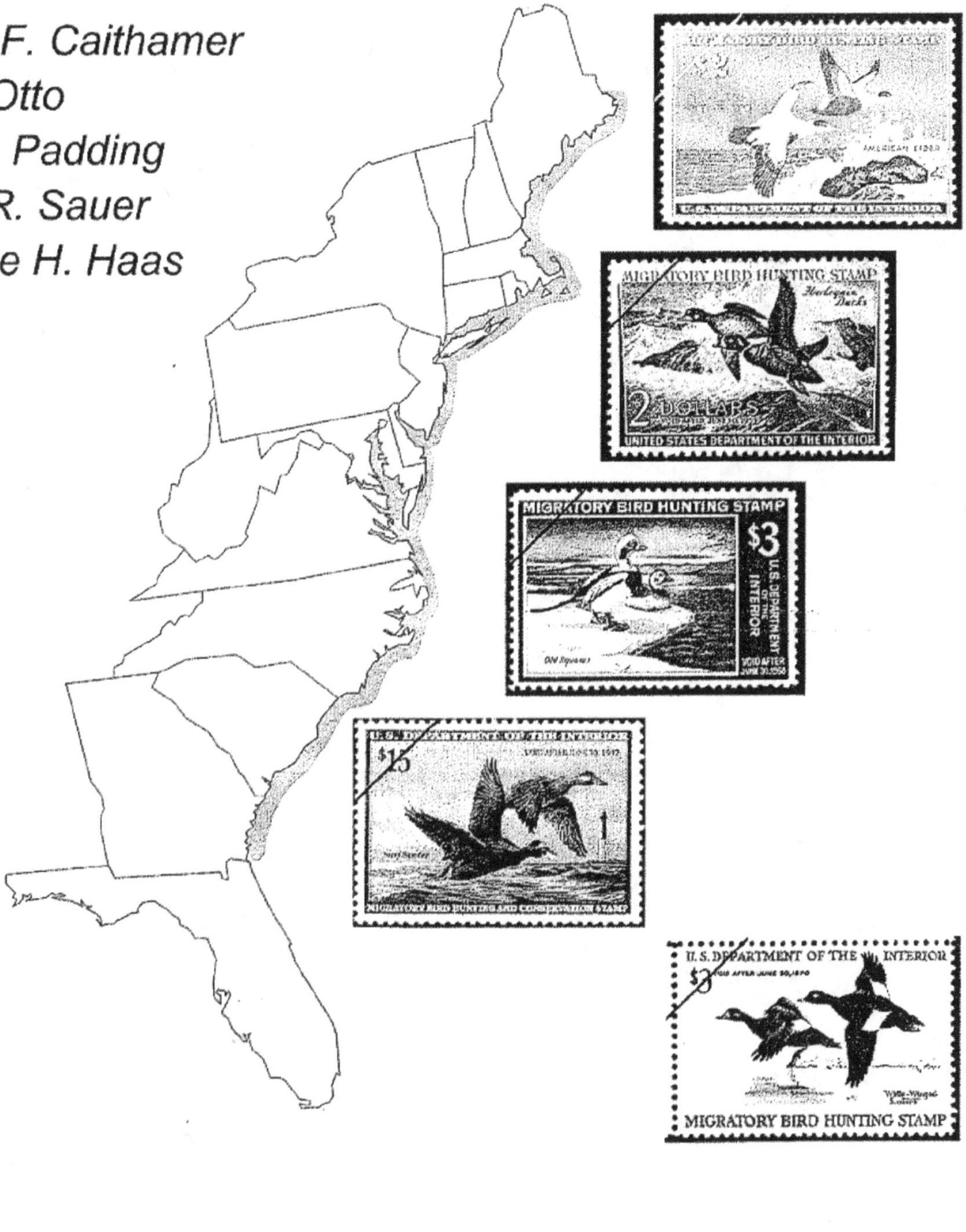

Sea Ducks in the Atlantic Flyway:
Population Status and a Review of Special Hunting Seasons

David F. Caithamer
Office of Migratory Bird Management
U.S. Fish and Wildlife Service
11500 American Holly Drive
Laurel, MD 20708-4016

Mark Otto
Office of Migratory Bird Management
U.S. Fish and Wildlife Service
11500 American Holly Drive
Laurel, MD 20708-4016

Paul I. Padding
Office of Migratory Bird Management
U.S. Fish and Wildlife Service
10815 Loblolly Pine Drive
Laurel, MD 20708-4028

John R. Sauer
Biological Resources Division
U.S. Geological Survey
11510 American Holly Drive
Laurel, MD 20708-4017

George H. Haas
U.S. Fish and Wildlife Service
300 Westgate Center Drive
Hadley, MA 01035-9589

February 2000

Sea Ducks in the Atlantic Flyway:
Population Status and a Review of Special Hunting Seasons

Executive Summary

Special seasons for sea ducks began in the Atlantic Flyway in 1938 when 5 northeastern states were allowed 16-30 day extensions to their regular duck seasons. Initially, only scoters were legal game during the extensions. Over time, the season became more liberal and by 1972, 13 of the 17 states in the Flyway had special seasons that lasted 107 days and had bag limits of 7 eiders, oldsquaws, and scoters in the aggregate. The Special Sea Duck Season in the Atlantic Flyway remained essentially unchanged until 1993, when a review of the status of sea ducks led to a reduction in the scoter bag limit to 4. Growing concern for the status of sea ducks and the need to evaluate the special season, especially the effects of restrictions on scoter bag limits, prompted our investigations.

We assessed trends in harvest and 4 long-term measures of sea duck abundance: (1) breeding population estimates from Canada and Alaska, (2) Christmas Bird Counts along the Atlantic Coast, (3) Mid-winter Inventory estimates from the Atlantic Flyway, and (4) Availability Indices (harvest/successful sea duck hunters) for the Flyway. We tested for changes in trends and levels that coincided with major changes in hunting regulations in the Flyway. In addition, we tested for annual changes in estimates of sea duck densities observed on the Atlantic Flyway Sea Duck Survey during 1991-97.

Harvest of oldsquaws, eiders, and scoters increased during 1963-71 as increasing numbers of states adopted the special season. Oldsquaw harvest remained stable during 1972-96, while harvest of eiders continued to increase. Scoter harvest declined during 1972-93, but appears to have stabilized since bag limits were restricted in 1993. We detected a decrease (64%) in the harvest of white-winged scoters coincident with bag limit restrictions, but detected no change in harvests of black scoters, surf scoters, and total scoters.

Numbers of common eider in the Atlantic Flyway appeared to have increased during 1972-97. Trends in indices of oldsquaw abundance were inconsistent for this period, but the index that we believe is most reliable reflected a stable population. Scoter population indices were stable or declining during 1972-92. Since 1993, we can only weakly infer stable or increasing populations for scoters.

We concluded that changes in hunting regulations in the Atlantic Flyway can produce measurable changes in harvest. However, we found only weak evidence that changes in population status coincided with changes in regulations. Nonetheless, we believe that mortality of sea ducks from hunting is nearly completely additive to natural mortality, considering the life-history characteristics of sea ducks. Although sea ducks have smaller harvests than many other waterfowl, conservative hunting regulations seem prudent considering our overall state of knowledge of these birds. We recommend consideration of a regular sea duck season that replaces the Special Sea Duck Season, and eliminating sea ducks from the regular duck season. We suggest eliminating provisions for special sea duck zones from the Federal framework of regulations.

We recommend that the Atlantic Flyway Council in cooperation with others develop a management plan for sea ducks. The plan should not be restricted to harvest management, but should address other issues and information needs. The plan should be developed in concert with the Sea Duck Joint Venture of the North American Waterfowl Management Plan. Lastly, we suggest a goal to maintain sea duck populations at or above levels observed during the 1970's.

Introduction

Concern over the status of sea ducks worldwide has increased in recent years. In North America, this concern relates to the limited state of knowledge of this group compared to many other waterfowl (Bellrose 1980, Goudie et al. 1994), reports of declining populations (Goudie 1989, Kertell 1991, Stehn et al. 1993, *Ad Hoc* Sea Duck Committee Atlantic Flyway Technical Section 1994), the potential impact that hunting may have on their status (Reed and Erskine 1986, *Ad Hoc* Sea Duck Committee Atlantic Flyway Technical Section 1994, Krementz et al. 1996, Krementz et al. 1997), and the susceptibility of these birds to catastrophic and chronic environmental degradation (Di Giulio and Scanlon 1984, Ohlendorf et al. 1986, Ohlendorf and Fleming 1988, Piatt et al. 1990, Franson et al. 1995). Our purpose was to assess population status and trends of sea ducks commonly found in coastal areas of the eastern U.S. The species we considered are oldsquaw (*Clangula hyemalis*), harlequin duck (*Histrionicus histrionicus*), common eider (*Somateria mollissima*), black scoter (*Melanitta nigra*), white-winged scoter (*M. fusca*), and surf scoter (*M. perspicillata*). We chose to not analyze data on king eider (*S. spectabilis*) because their wintering range barely extends into the U.S. portion of the Atlantic Flyway.

Sea ducks are hunted in the Atlantic Flyway during regular duck and Special Sea Duck Seasons. The Special Sea Duck Seasons have never been reviewed and evaluated since their inception in 1938, although the status of sea ducks in eastern North America was evaluated in 1993 and 1994 (Office of Migratory Bird Management 1993, *Ad Hoc* Sea Duck Committee Atlantic Flyway Technical Section 1994). Those assessments revealed mostly decreasing trends in indices of scoter populations, stable or increasing trends in indices of common eider populations, and stable or decreasing trends in indices of oldsquaw populations. Based largely on these findings, the USFWS and Atlantic Flyway Council agreed in 1993 to restrict bag limits of scoters during Special Sea Duck Seasons in the Atlantic Flyway. USFWS policy states that special seasons "may be re-evaluated for their effectiveness, appropriateness and necessity when situations (are) warranted" (U.S. Fish and Wildlife Service 1988). In addition to assessing the status and trends of sea duck populations, we also assess impacts of recent restrictions on scoter bag limits and other impacts of special seasons on scoter, eider, and oldsquaw populations.

We retrospectively described and examined trends in estimates of harvest, the ratios of young per adult duck in the harvest, and indices of breeding and wintering populations. We searched for correlation between changes in hunting regulations and changes in estimates of harvest and indices of population size. Our analyses focused on data that were most pertinent to the U.S. portion of the Atlantic Flyway.

We thank G. T. Allen, A. W. Brackney, J. P. Bladen, R. E. Cummins, K. M. Dickson, B. A. Hoover, P. D. Keywood, R. J. King, and J. R. Serie for assistance. Biologists from states and provinces in the Atlantic Flyway provided information on hunting seasons within their jurisdiction. The Wildlife Management Institute graciously allowed reproductions of figures from Bellrose (1980). Numerous other persons and agencies supplied data via support for, or participation in, various wildlife management activities and surveys.

History of sea duck hunting regulations in the Atlantic Flyway

Since adoption of the Migratory Bird Treaty Act in 1918, sea duck hunting regulations in the Atlantic Flyway have become progressively more liberal and complex (Appendix 1). Sea duck harvests were regulated through regular duck season limits from 1918 through 1937 in all states of the Flyway. During most of this period (1918-31), the season was closed for eiders. In 1938, a Special Sea Duck Season was established for Maine, New Hampshire, Connecticut, Massachusetts, and Rhode Island. This season, during which scoters could be taken "in open coastal waters only, beyond outer harbor lines," was open from September 15 until opening day of the regular duck season. The daily bag and possession limits during this special season were the same as those for the regular duck season. Other than changes in the length of the special season due to changes in opening dates of the regular duck seasons, those regulations remained the same during 1938-46, except for the addition of a special season in New York, including Long Island, in 1940. During 1938-46, the length of the sea duck season was 5-20 days in Maine and New Hampshire, and 16-41 days in Connecticut, Massachusetts, New York, and Rhode Island.

Regular duck seasons were reduced from 45 days in 1946 to 24 (Maine, New Hampshire, and New York) or 30 (Connecticut, Massachusetts, and Rhode Island) days in 1947, and daily bag limits were reduced from 7 ducks in 1946 to 4 in 1947. This appears to have led to an expansion of sea duck seasons beginning in 1947; New Hampshire (36 days, opening on September 1), Connecticut (63 days), Massachusetts (63 days), and Rhode Island (77 days) had special seasons prior to their regular seasons, whereas Maine (72 days) and New York (89 days)

5

had sea duck seasons that began before and extended through their regular seasons. Also, bag limits for sea ducks were separated from limits for other ducks at this time; the daily bag and possession limits for sea ducks seasons was 7 and 14 scoters, respectively. In 1948, eiders were included in the legal bag for Special Sea Duck Seasons, and oldsquaw was added in 1950. Connecticut was allowed an additional 6-day late season immediately after the end of its 1948 regular season, and in 1949 and 1950, all 6 states had 92-day special seasons from September 17 through December 17. During 1951-57, season dates and lengths were state-specific, with opening dates of September 14 - October 17 and closing dates of December 29 - January 5.

Sea duck season dates remained standardized for all participating states during 1958-72. The seasons ranged from 100-108 days in length, opened in late September or early October, and closed in early or mid-January. A significant change in sea duck hunting regulations was made in 1960; all states in the Atlantic Flyway were allowed "in addition to the bag limit on other ducks, a daily bag limit of 7 and a possession limit of 14 eider, old-squaw (sic), and scoter ducks, singly or in the aggregate of these species" during the regular duck season.

During 1963-71, existing sea duck zones were expanded and the number of states offering Special Sea Duck Seasons increased from 6 to 13. Sea duck zones in Connecticut, Maine, Massachusetts, New Hampshire, and Rhode Island were redefined in 1963 as "all coastal waters and all waters of rivers and streams lying seaward from the first upstream bridge," with similar but more detailed area-specific zone descriptions for New York. Maryland, New Jersey, and North Carolina were allowed Special Sea Duck Seasons beginning in 1966, "in any waters of the Atlantic Ocean and/or in any tidal waters of any bay which are separated by at least 1 mile of open water from any shore, island, and emergent vegetation: provided, that any such areas have been described, delineated, and designated as special sea duck areas under the hunting regulations adopted by the respective States." Georgia, Virginia, and South Carolina were allowed Special Sea Duck Seasons under the same guidelines in 1968, as was Delaware in 1971. The minimum allowable distance from any shore, island, or emergent vegetation was apparently intended to protect riparian landowner rights, reduce disturbance of other waterfowl, and avoid competition between sea duck hunters and waterfowl hunters using stationary blinds (Stotts 1966, L. Hindman, Md. Wildlife Heritage Div., pers. commun.). This distance was reduced to 1200 yards in Maryland in 1969 and 800 yards in 1970; by 1975, the prescribed distance for Delaware, North Carolina and Virginia was also 800 yards (Fig. 1).

From 1973 to 1997, more general frameworks have been used for Special Sea Duck Seasons and regulations have remained relatively similar from year to year. In 1973, framework dates were established at September 1 - January 20, season length at 107 days, and bag and possession limits at 7 and 14, respectively. The opening framework date was changed from September 1 to September 16-18 during 1976-1978, and to September 15 during 1979-1997. The flyway-wide "bonus bag" of sea ducks during the regular season ended in 1987, when eiders, oldsquaw, and scoters became part of the overall duck bag in all areas except designated sea duck zones. In sea duck zones, however, hunters could still take a limit of sea ducks in addition to a bag of other ducks during the regular season. The season on harlequin ducks was closed in the Atlantic Flyway in 1989, and has remained closed since then. In 1993, the daily bag limit on scoters was reduced to 4, while the aggregate bag limit on eiders, oldsquaws, and scoters remained at 7. These bag limits have been used in Special Sea Duck Seasons of the Atlantic Flyway since then.

In 1997, states that prohibited hunting on Sundays were allowed additional waterfowl hunting days to compensate for Sunday closures. Sea duck seasons in Delaware, Maine, New Jersey, and North Carolina encompassed 112-125 days, although the number of hunting days remained ≤107 days. Other states eligible for "compensatory days" did not use them to extend sea duck seasons.

Natural History

Oldsquaw

No subspecies of oldsquaw are recognized (Sibley and Monroe 1990). They nest circumpolarly in tundra habitat near coastlines, lakes, and ponds and winter along the Pacific and Atlantic coasts and in the Great Lakes of North America (Fig. 2) (Johnsgard 1978, Bellrose 1980). Oldsquaws usually form their first pair bonds in their second winter and attempt nesting the following spring (Johnsgard 1978, Bellrose 1980). Pair bonds generally last only through the nesting period, although some females will pair with the same male in successive years (Alison 1975, Johnsgard 1978, Bellrose 1980, Oring and Sayler 1992). Philopatry to nesting areas can be strong, as some nesting pairs return to the same pond in successive years (Alison 1975, Bellrose 1980). Clutch size averages 6-7 eggs and incubation lasts about 26 days (Alison 1975, Johnsgard

1978, Bellrose 1980). Nest success averaged 59% and no renesting was observed in one study near Churchill, Manitoba (Alison 1975). Males leave their mates during incubation (Alison 1975, Johnsgard 1978, Bellrose 1980, Oring and Sayler 1992). Females occasionally abandon their brood to begin the postnuptial molt, which can lead to amalgamations of several broods without parents (Johnsgard 1978, Bellrose 1980). Most adult males migrate to molting areas for the summer wing molt (Salomonsen 1968, Hohman et al. 1992). Young oldsquaws require only 35 days to attain flight (Johnsgard 1978, Bellrose 1980). Oldsquaws feed primarily on crustaceans and mollusks (Cottam 1939, Stott and Olson 1973, Johnsgard 1978, Bellrose 1980).

Harlequin Duck

No subspecies of harlequin ducks are recognized (Sibley and Monroe 1990). In North America, the range of harlequins appears discontinuous (Fig. 2) and is assumed to be comprised of 2 distinct populations (Bellrose 1980, Cassirer et al. 1991). In the east, birds nest from Greenland south to the Gulf of St. Lawrence, and winter in coastal areas from Greenland southward to the Chesapeake Bay (Bellrose 1980, Vickery 1988). Recent studies have demonstrated that some harlequins move between Greenland and Quebec (P. Laporte, Can. Wildlife Service, pers. commun.). In the west, harlequins range from Alaska southward to California. The western population is much larger than the eastern population (Bellrose 1980). Harlequin ducks were listed as endangered in eastern Canada in 1991. Harlequins typically nest on rocky shorelines of turbulent mountainous rivers and spend the winter along rocky ocean coastlines (Bellrose 1980). They probably form their first pair bonds late in their second winter and are not known to nest until they are 2 years old (Johnsgard 1975, Bellrose 1980). Some pairs may remain paired for more than one year or re-pair repeatedly (Oring and Sayler 1992). Clutch size averages 5-6 eggs (Bengtson 1965, Jarvis and Bruner 1996) and incubation lasts 28-30 days (Bengtson 1965, Johnstone 1970). Little information is available on nest success, time required for young to attain flight, and post-breeding movements of adults (Bellrose 1980). Harlequin ducks eat mostly crustaceans, mollusks, and insects (Cottam 1939).

Common Eider

Common eiders have a circumpolar distribution in the Northern Hemisphere (Fig. 3) (Bellrose 1980). Sibley and Monroe (1990) recognize 2 subspecies of common eider in North

America, while Bellrose (1980) and Johnsgard (1978) recognize 4; we accept the classification of Bellrose and Johnsgard. The American eider (*Somareria mollissima dresseri*) is the only race typically encountered in the eastern U.S. They breed in coastal areas from Massachusetts to southern Labrador, and spend winters in coastal waters from the Gulf of St. Lawrence to New Jersey. American eiders have recovered from extremely low numbers of the late 1800's (Krohn et al. 1992). At various times, adult eiders and eggs have been transplanted to potential nesting sites (Heusmann 1995). The other North American races are found in Hudson and James bays (*S. m. sedentaria*), western Canada and Alaska (*S. m. v-nigra*), and northeastern Canada and Greenland (*S. m. borealis*) (Bellrose 1980) (Fig. 3). All races utilize coastal marine habitats extensively. Common eiders form pairs in their second or later winter (Spurr and Milne 1976). Common eiders are seasonally monogamous and some may reestablish pair bonds with previous mates (Spurr and Milne 1976, Bellrose 1980). American eiders do not breed until they are at least 3 years old (Mendall 1968). Female eiders rely extensively on nutrient reserves acquired before nesting to lay and incubate a clutch of eggs (Korschgen 1977). They commonly nest in colonies on islands where many females return to their same nesting site in successive years (Cooch 1965, Johnsgard 1975, Bellrose 1980). Clutch sizes are typically 4 or 5, and incubation lasts about 26 days (Korschgen 1977, Bellrose 1980, van Dijk 1986). If their nest is destroyed, some females will renest (Cooch 1965, Korschgen 1977). Multiple broods and females often coalesce into crèches (Munro and Bédard 1977, Prach et al. 1986). Predation rate of flightless young can exceed 90% in some areas (Mendenhall and Milne 1985, Mawhinney and Diamond 1997). Young require about 60 days to be capable of flight (Cooch 1965). Some eiders migrate to molting areas (Abraham and Finney 1986). Mollusks, especially blue mussels, crustaceans, and other invertebrates are important foods to common eiders (Cottam 1939).

Black Scoter

Two subspecies of black scoters are recognized; the American black scoter (*M. n. americana*) is found in North America (Sibley and Monroe 1990). Its nesting range includes Alaska, the lowlands near Hudson Bay, and other areas across Canada (Fig. 3) (Johnsgard 1975, Bellrose 1980, Savard and Lamothe 1991). Black scoters spend the winters in salty or brackish waters along the Pacific and Atlantic coasts. Pairs are first formed during their second winter and nesting is attempted the following spring. Little is known about nesting of black scoters in

North America (Johnsgard 1978, Bellrose 1980). Apparently, males leave their mates when incubation begins (Johnsgard 1975, Bordage and Savard 1995). On the Yukon Delta of Alaska, black scoter clutch sizes range from 5 to 8 eggs (Brandt 1943 cited by Bellrose 1980). In Iceland, initial clutches average 9 eggs, and clutches of renesting scoters average 6 eggs (Johnsgard 1978). However, Bellrose (1980) believes that renesting is uncommon among black scoters in North America. Incubation lasts 27-28 days and brood mixing is not typical (Johnsgard 1978). It probably takes 6-7 weeks for young to achieve flight (Johnsgard 1978, Bellrose 1980). In North America and Europe, black scoters migrate to molting areas during the summer (Salomonsen 1968, Bellrose 1980, Hohman et al. 1992, Bordage and Savard 1995). Black scoters eat mostly mollusks, crustaceans, and other invertebrates (Cottam 1939, Stott and Olson 1973, Johnsgard 1975).

White-winged Scoter

Three subspecies of white-winged scoter are recognized (Sibley and Monroe 1990). The American white-winged scoter (*M. f. deglandi*) is found in North America where it breeds primarily in coniferous forest and parkland habitats of Alaska and western Canada (Fig. 4) (Johnsgard 1975, Bellrose 1980, although see Savard and Lamothe 1991). However, their breeding range has apparently contracted northward since the late 1940's (*Ad Hoc* Sea Duck Committee Atlantic Flyway Technical Section 1994). White-winged scoters winter in salty and brackish habitats along the Pacific and Atlantic coasts (Johnsgard 1975, Bellrose 1980). Like black scoters, white-winged scoters are seasonally monogamous and they do not pair or attempt to breed until their second year (Johnsgard 1975, Bellrose 1980, Brown and Houston 1982). Females often return to the same nesting site in successive years (Brown and Brown 1981). In southern portions of their breeding range, their clutch size averages about 9 eggs and the nesting success rate averages about 70% (Brown and Brown 1981, Brown and Fredrickson 1989). Bellrose (1980) believes that renesting is uncommon in white-winged scoters. Many females abandon their broods within the first few weeks after hatch and the ducklings aggregate into crèches that are accompanied by variable numbers of adult females (Brown and Brown 1981, Kehoe 1989). Young scoters require 63-77 days to attain flight (Hochbaum 1944, Brown and Fredrickson 1997). Adults commonly migrate to molting areas in the summer (Salomonsen 1968, Johnson and Richardson 1982, Brown and Fredrickson 1989). Young and adult scoters in central Saskatchewan feed primarily on amphipods during the summer (Brown and Fredrickson 1986). On wintering areas, they eat mostly mollusks, crustaceans, and other invertebrates (Cottam 1939, Stott and Olson 1973).

Surf Scoter

No subspecies of surf scoter are recognized (Sibley and Monroe 1990). They breed in boreal forests of Alaska and Canada and winter in brackish and salty waters along the Atlantic and Pacific coasts (Fig. 4) (Bellrose 1980, also see Reed et al. 1994). Surf scoters are probably seasonally monogamous and first pair and breed at the end of their second year (Johnsgard 1975). Average clutch size is probably 5-7 eggs (Bent 1925). Little is known about nesting success of surf scoters and length of time required for young to be capable of flight (Bellrose 1980). In a southern portion of its breeding range, crèching behavior seems common (Reed et al. 1994). Adults migrate to molting areas (Johnson and Richardson 1982, Salter et al. 1980). Mollusks and crustaceans are important foods during winter while insects are more important to juveniles in summer (Cottam 1939, Stott and Olson 1973).

METHODS

Data Collection

Harvest and Recruitment Index.— Recreational harvest of ducks in the U.S. is annually estimated by the U.S. Fish and Wildlife Service through a questionnaire survey of Federal duck stamp purchasers (Martin and Carney 1977). Survey respondents report the number of days they hunted waterfowl and the number of sea ducks, other ducks, geese, and coots they bagged in each state in which they hunted waterfowl. Combined with a complete count of the number of Federal duck stamps sold, results of this survey provide estimates of the total U.S. harvest of sea ducks and other waterfowl. The survey also provides estimates of the number of active waterfowl hunters in each state and the number of days they hunted waterfowl, but it does not provide any estimate of hunter activity specific to sea duck hunting. The estimated number of successful sea duck hunters is the only index of sea duck hunting effort that is available from this survey.

The U.S. Fish and Wildlife Service also conducts an annual waterfowl parts survey, the sample for which consists of hunters who reported bagging ≥1 duck, goose, or coot during the

11

previous hunting season (Martin and Carney 1977). Respondents are asked to send a wing from every duck and coot they bag and the tail feathers of each goose they bag, and to report the state, county, and date of harvest for each bird. Biologists can determine the species, sex, and age (immature or adult) of a duck from its wing plumage (Carney 1992). Thus, sea duck wings received through this survey, combined with estimates of the total sea duck harvest, provide estimates of the species, sex, and age composition as well as the geographic and temporal distribution of the sea duck harvest in the U.S. The precision of these estimates is dependent on the number of hunters responding to the questionnaire survey and the number of wings received. The U.S. Fish and Wildlife Service does not estimate the variances of its estimates, but they are probably large for sea ducks harvest estimates, especially at the state level. Precision of the U.S. Fish and Wildlife Service harvest estimates diminishes for species with small harvests, such as sea duck species, and for smaller geographic areas (Geissler 1990).

The Canadian Wildlife Service similarly estimates sport harvest in Canada (Cooch et al. 1978). Canada's National Harvest Survey consists of a questionnaire, sent to a sample of current and previous-year national migratory bird permit purchasers, that asks hunters to report how many days they hunted migratory birds and how many ducks, geese, and other migratory game birds they bagged. Responses to this survey coupled with counts of total migratory bird permits sold provide estimates of the number of active migratory bird hunters, the number of days they hunted, and the number of ducks, geese, and other migratory game birds harvested in Canada. As in the United States, the National Harvest Survey includes an annual parts survey that enables the Canadian Wildlife Service to estimate the species, sex, and age composition of Canada's waterfowl harvest.

Breeding Population.—Annual indices to the size of scoter, eider, and oldsquaw breeding populations are obtained from an aerial survey across much of Canada, Alaska, and the northcentral U.S. (Appendix 2) (Canadian Wildlife Service and U.S. Fish and Wildlife Service 1987, Smith 1995). The Breeding Waterfowl and Habitat Survey (hereafter called Breeding Waterfowl Survey) is directed primarily at mallards and does not provide complete coverage of the breeding ranges of some sea ducks. The survey generally begins in early May in southern strata and finishes by mid-June in northern areas. Protocol for this survey does not require identifying species of eiders or scoters, except since 1998 in Alaska. Here, species of scoters is identified when they are located within 100 m of the transect center-line. Data on harlequin ducks are pooled with several other species.

Aerial estimates are adjusted for visibility bias. Visibility adjustments for southern areas are determined annually through concurrent ground counts, while those for northern strata were determined through concurrent helicopter counts that were conducted in 1986-91. These helicopter-based visibility adjustment rates for northern strata have been used for all years of the survey. However, the visibility of waterfowl improved dramatically in Alaska and the Yukon Territory (strata 1-12) beginning in 1977 due to a change in the type of airplane used for surveys (Hodges et al. 1996). Thus, visibility adjustments determined in 1986-91 may be biased low for pre-1977 estimates in Alaska and the Yukon Territory.

This survey became operational in most strata in 1955. However, it was not operational in Alaska and the Yukon Territory until 1957, and in eastern Canada (strata 51-57, and 62-69) not until 1990 or later. Because a large proportion of the total sea duck population is found in Alaska, and because data from only a few years are available from eastern Canada, we chose to restrict our analyses to data from strata 1-50 and 75-77 (Traditional Survey Area) during the years 1957-97.

Mid-winter Inventory.—Waterfowl populations in states of the Atlantic Flyway are annually surveyed by the Mid-winter Inventory (MWI), which is a series of coordinated aerial and ground counts conducted in early January (Martin et al. 1979, Eggeman and Johnson 1989). Survey coverage of the MWI typically includes inland and near-shore habitats, but not deepwater areas of the ocean that often harbor large numbers of sea ducks. This survey has been criticized because of inconsistent methodology across regions and time (Montalbano et al. 1985, Eggeman and Johnson 1989). Because this survey does not extend northward into Canada, variable numbers of sea ducks wintering in Canada are uncounted. Data are not tabulated separately for each species of scoter and eider. Despite these limitations, results from mid-winter surveys have been found to reflect changes in the size of other duck populations (Conroy et al. 1988), and we believe that they may also reveal large and long-term changes in numbers of sea ducks.

Christmas Bird Counts (CBC).— This annual survey of birds across North America is coordinated by the National Audubon Society (Butcher 1990, Sauer et al. 1996). Counts of birds are collected in sample units (circles) that are 15 miles in diameter. On a selected day within 2 weeks of 25 December, volunteers search the predefined area, and record all birds encountered.

Most birds are identified to species, but occasionally the species is not determined. For example, some counts are recorded for unidentified scoters. The number of circles surveyed in North America increased from 512 in 1955 to 1644 in 1995. The number of participants varied greatly among circles in any year and within circles over time. Survey effort varied from a mean of 40.8 party-hours per circle in 1955 to 70.4 hours per circle in 1995. Consequently, analyses of these data must include some adjustment for varying effort, and the exact form of the adjustment is often not evident from the data (Butcher 1990.) In earlier years, most counts were located in coastal areas or near large cities, and circles were developed by local coordinators rather than placed within a sampling frame. Although some coastal areas are surveyed, there have been no consistent surveys of areas offshore. The results therefore do not provide statistical samples of absolute abundance. Despite these limitations, we believe that CBC may be useful as long-term indices to changes in sizes of sea duck populations.

Sea Duck Survey.—Aerial surveys designed to estimate the density of sea ducks in coastal habitats were conducted during late January and early February of 1991, 1992, 1994, 1995, and 1997-99. Sea ducks were counted from airplanes flying over predetermined transects centered approximately 500 meters offshore and parallel to the coast. Transects were 500 meters wide and divided into segments that were 10 nautical miles long. Survey coverage extended from southern Georgia northward to New Brunswick and Nova Scotia. Approximately 440 flight segments were surveyed in each of the years by 2 crews. During 1991 and 1992, < 50% of the scoters were identified to species; in other years > 98% of the scoter were identified to species.

Bandings and Band Recoveries.—We obtained electronic data files of all sea duck bandings and band recoveries from the Bird Banding Laboratory of the U.S. Geological Survey in September, 1997. Total numbers of bandings and recoveries were tabulated, and banding and recovery locations were plotted on maps. No maps were made for black and surf scoters because there were fewer than 15 band recoveries for each of these species.

Analyses

Time Series Analyses of Breeding Waterfowl Survey, MWI, Harvest, Age Composition, and Availability Indices.—We modeled and tested for different linear trends in annual estimates of breeding populations, mid-winter populations, harvest, and in an index of availability. The Availability Index is the estimated harvest divided by the estimated number of successful sea duck hunters. For age composition of the harvest, we had no hypotheses to test, so we only plotted a locally weighted regression (lowess) curve (Cleveland 1979) of each time series. Age composition of the harvest is the proportion of immatures (immature ducks harvested/total ducks harvested). Lowess is a robust regression that uses nearby time points to calculate each smoothed value or prediction. We used Auto-Regressive-Integrated-Moving-Average (ARIMA) time series analytical methods (Box and Jenkins 1970) to test for lack of independence in the regression errors and to model the correlation over time (Appendix 3). We obtained valid statistical tests of selected hypotheses by jointly modeling the linear regression terms and the ARIMA time series errors (Box and Jenkins 1970, Time Series Staff of Census Bureau Statistical Research Division 1995). We used an alpha-level of 0.05, unless specified otherwise.

We tested hypotheses that changes in sea duck hunting regulations in the Atlantic Flyway would effect trends in estimates of harvest and population indices (Table 1). These regulatory periods varied some by species. For oldsquaw, the periods were 1956-62, with relatively stable and conservative regulations; 1963-71, when regulations became increasingly liberal; and 1972-96, with relatively stable and liberal regulations. The regulatory periods for scoters were similar to those for oldsquaw, except that a restrictive period was implemented beginning in 1993. Thus the periods for scoters were 1956-62 (relatively stable and conservative), 1963-71 (increasingly liberal), 1972-1992 (stable and liberal), and 1993-96 (stable and moderate). Population responses were expected to lag behind regulatory changes (e.g., a change in hunting regulations in the fall of 1993 would change the 1994 breeding population estimate). We evaluated interval-specific population changes using a procedure similar to piecewise linear regression. Regulations for eider hunting have remained relatively stable in Maine, Massachusetts, Connecticut, and New Hampshire. Since 1953, the eider season has been 100-108 days with a 7 bird daily limit in these 4 states. Because eider regulations were stable there, and because these states account for >99% of the eider harvest in the Atlantic Flyway, we had no opportunity to assess the impacts of regulatory changes on eider harvest or population status.

In our analyses of time series data, we: (1) checked for nonstationarity or changes in the variance over time and against the size of the estimate; (2) checked for nonstationarity or changes in the level of the series; (3) conducted stepwise backward elimination to choose the significant regression effects; (4) modeled the time series structure of the regression errors; (5) identified point and level-shift outliers; (6) verified that the final regression plus time series model was appropriate with no systematic patterns in residuals and no large autocorrelations; and (7) graphically compared regression predictions to estimates produced through lowess smoothing techniques (Cleveland 1979).

To check for nonstationarity in variance, we plotted each series over time and looked for systematic changes in variability. Estimates of breeding population, mid-winter population, harvest, and age ratio were modeled using the log-transformed values because the variance increased with the level of the estimates. When checking breeding population estimates, which had associated estimates of sampling error, we also plotted the cube root of the sampling error variances against the survey estimates and again against the model predictions as suggested by Carroll and Ruppert (1988). We used log-transformations of the breeding population estimates because of the positive relation between sample errors to the original estimates. Next we plotted the logged-transformed series against its sampling error, the relative variance (variance/mean^2). These plots revealed no relation, suggesting this was a proper transformation. After transforming the data, we verified that there were no patterns of variability over time.

We checked for nonstationarity in the level of the series by adjusting the series with all the possible regression variables and checking autocorrelation statistics in the regression residuals. If the autocorrelations diminished more slowly than the rate of exponential decay, then the data were not stationary. No evidence of nonstationarity in the levels was found in any of the series. Stationarity was important because reporting overall means is only meaningful if the data are stationary. Also, we then could fit simple stationary autoregressive (AR) or moving-average (MA) models.

Next, out of all the possible periods of population change hypothesized (modeled by slope parameters called "ramps" and interventions called "level-shifts") (Table 1), we used stepwise backward elimination to evaluate models with different combinations of slopes and level-shifts. We retained models where all regression variables were significant (Draper and Smith 1981). Estimating the time series and the regression parameters jointly required testing of some non-nested models, so we used the difference in the bias-corrected version of the Akaike's Information Criterion (AIC) (Hurvich and Tsai 1989) to test for significant differences between models. A variable was also removed if the AIC did not increase. We conducted the backward elimination process manually and checked for outliers and for changes in ARIMA time series error structure at several points in the elimination process. Changes might have indicated that an important feature in the regression was being removed. These rarely occurred.

We identified point and level-shift outliers with an automated procedure (Time Series Staff of Census Bureau Statistical Research Division 1995). Because of the large number of tests that were conducted during the process, we used a critical t-value of 3.8 corresponding to an experiment-wise p-value of 0.01 in the tests (R. Templeton, Statistics New Zealand, pers. commun.). We investigated the validity of outliers and excluded from models those that we believed were due to deviations from standard data collection procedures.

After we determined the final set of regression variables, we again checked plots of the regression residuals for systematic differences over time and variability with the level of the residuals. We also plotted the cube root of the survey sample variances against the regression or model predictions. This is similar to the diagnostic methods we used earlier to look for nonstationarity in variances of raw samples.

In addition to modeling linear changes over time, we used lowess regression with a high smoothing value ($f= 0.67$) to describe each time series. We checked our modeling results against lowess estimates, expecting similar slopes from both the linear and lowess regressions. However, when analyzing age composition data we relied exclusively on lowess regressions, since we had no *a priori* hypotheses regarding change in these data.

We evaluated possible visibility differences for breeding population estimates from Alaska and the Yukon Territory (strata 1-12) prior to 1977 (Hodges et al. 1996). Since the change in visibility was not estimated directly by comparing simultaneous counts from new and old aircraft in 1977, we tested models that included a level shift in 1977 and assumed that changes in levels of breeding populations between 1963-76 and 1977-96 were due to improved visibility of waterfowl in the more recent period. We modeled the log-transformed population estimates, and then used the regression coefficients as multiplicative correction factors for the pre-1977 estimates.

Christmas Bird Count.— Data from 1955-95 were provided by the Patuxent Wildlife Research Center (B. A. Hoover, Patuxent Wildlife Research Center, Personal Communication). We analyzed data from the 6 species of interest and for all scoters combined, which included unidentified scoters. Data on unidentified eiders were excluded. We calculated population year effects (composite yearly indices of abundance) and estimates of trend using the methods in Link and Sauer (1998, 1999). In this procedure, a generalized linear model is used with effort adjustments of form (ξ^{p}), where ξ is the effort at a site. The size of the exponent p determines the form of the effort adjustment. Link and Sauer (1999) developed a method for estimating p in which the model is fit with alternative values of p, and the value of p that produces the model with smallest deviance is used in future modeling. Once p is chosen (i.e., the appropriate form of the effort adjustment is specified), the significance of the overall effort adjustment is accessed by determining whether the coefficient of the effort adjustment is different from 0.

Once the need for effort adjustments was assessed for each species, the generalized linear model with year effects and appropriate effort adjustments was fit for 10 regions (groups of states and provinces in Atlantic Flyway). Estimated regional abundances were also calculated using the appropriate effort adjustments, and were standardized to a consistent year using the estimated year effects. Year effects were combined among regions using empirical Bayes procedures as suggested in Link and Sauer (1998). In these procedures, differences in precision of regional year effects are accommodated by replacing them with a weighted average of the original time series and a composite time series, and weights are determined by the relative precision of the original time series. These averaged time series are then weighted by relative abundances and areas within regions to estimate year effects for the entire population.

Population trends were estimated as a linear regression through the year effects at the regional level, accommodating for covariances among year effects. These trends were then averaged among regions using the empirical Bayes procedures and weightings described above.

We determined trends for the Atlantic Coast, which we defined to include all states of the Atlantic Flyway, plus New Brunswick, Nova Scotia, Ontario, Prince Edward Island, and Quebec.

We evaluated population changes during several periods that corresponded with changes in hunting regulations (Table 1). For harlequin ducks we evaluated 2 different periods: 1955-89 when hunting was permitted in the Atlantic Flyway, and 1990-95 when no hunting was allowed. We used one-sided t-tests to evaluate null hypotheses of no differences in population trends between periods. Alternative hypotheses were that trends would be lower (less positive) in periods with more liberal regulations. For example, alternative hypotheses for comparisons of trends from 1955-63 and 1964-72 were that trends would be lower in the later period because of liberalizations in regulations. Alternative hypotheses for comparisons of 1964-72 and 1973-93 were that trends would be lower in the later period when regulations were the most liberal. For the comparison of scoter trends between 1973-93 and 1994-95, our alternative hypotheses were that trends would be higher in the later period when scoter bag limits were restricted.

Sea Duck Survey.—We used a simpler approach for analyzing data from the sea duck survey because data from only 7 years were available. We tested for linear trends in annual totals of each species.

RESULTS

Bandings and Band Recoveries

Numbers of sea duck band recoveries generally are inadequate to test hypothesis on the presence of regional populations using multiresponse permutation procedures (Mielke et al. 1981, Slauson et al. 1991, Krementz et al. 1996) (Table 2). However, recovery locations of common eiders, oldsquaws, harlequins, and white-winged scoters (Fig. 5) do not refute the possibility of regional populations (Reed and Erskine 1986, Cassirer et al. 1991, Canadian Wildlife Service et al. 1997) or reference areas where members of a population share similar population parameters (Krementz et al. 1996). Most band recoveries of common eider in the Atlantic Flyway are from birds banded in areas along the Atlantic Coast. Oldsquaw banded near Cape Churchill, Manitoba have only been recovered in the Great Lakes, Chesapeake Bay, or near the banding location. Oldsquaws banded in Alaska have never been recovered in the Atlantic Flyway. Recovery locations of harlequins in western North America tend to be near areas where they were banded. Many recoveries of white-winged scoter bands along the Pacific Coast were from those banded in Alberta; however, some white-winged scoters banded in Alberta also were recovered along the Atlantic Coast.

Harvest Estimates

Successful Sea Duck Hunters.—The number of successful sea duck hunters increased during 1965-1972 as more states were allowed sea duck seasons, but appears to have declined since 1974 (Fig. 6). The decline coincided with a more rapid decrease in active waterfowl hunters in the Atlantic Flyway during the same period (Martin and Padding 1997).

U.S. and Canadian Harvests.—On average, the number of sea ducks harvested in the Eastern Provinces of Canada was similar to the number harvested in the states of the Atlantic

Flyway and has totaled about 154,500 per year (Appendix 4). On an annual basis, the proportion of the total harvest that occurred in each country has varied considerably. For example, only 35% of the total sea duck harvest occurred in the U.S. in 1980, while in 1991, 65% occurred there. This pattern of annual variation, but overall similar harvest between the Canadian and U.S. regions was evident for all the commonly harvested species. Only king eiders and harlequins tended to be harvested in greater numbers in Canada, but the harvest of both of these species was relatively low (<500 birds per year).

Spatial and Temporal Patterns.—From 1987-96, the mean annual harvest of oldsquaw during the Special Sea Duck Season was 13,500 birds, most of which were bagged in Maryland (50%), New York (18%), and Maine (17%) (Fig. 7). Almost all (98%) of the harvest occurred in special sea duck zones except in New York, where 28% of the oldsquaw were harvested from other areas (mostly Lake Erie and Lake Ontario). Oldsquaws were harvested primarily from November through the end of the hunting season (Fig. 7).

Almost all of the mean annual harvest of 25,500 common eiders occurred in Maine (51%) and Massachusetts (46%) (Fig. 7), and virtually all (99%) of the eiders harvested were bagged in special sea duck zones. Across the Flyway, harvest increased gradually as the season progressed (Fig. 7).

About 6,000 black scoters were harvested annually, with Maryland (37%), North Carolina (18%), and New York (13%) accounting for most of the birds bagged (Fig. 8). Only 12% of New York's harvest was in special sea duck zones, compared to 97% for the rest of the Flyway. More than half of the black scoters harvested were bagged in October (Fig. 8).

Hunters in New York (31%), Massachusetts (24%), Maine (14%), and Maryland (14%) bagged most of the 10,500 white-winged scoters harvested annually (Fig. 8). Almost all (99%) of the harvest occurred in special sea duck zones, except in New York (79%). The temporal distribution of the Flyway-wide harvest showed a peak in mid-October followed by a gradual decline through the rest of the season (Fig. 8).

The mean annual harvest of 12,000 surf scoters was more evenly distributed among states (Fig. 9). Maryland hunters bagged 35% of the total, while Massachusetts (16%), Maine (14%), New York (9%), and North Carolina (9%) each accounted for >1,000 surf scoters bagged annually. About 75% of New York's harvest occurred in special sea duck zones, compared to

98% for the rest of the Flyway. Most of the surf scoters harvested were taken during October and November (Fig. 9).

Maine, Massachusetts and Maryland together account for most of the Flyway's total sea duck harvest (Fig. 9). Across the Flyway, there is no clear peak in timing of harvest (Fig. 9).

Trends in Harvest.—Harvest trends are shown in Fig. 10-12 and annual rates of change are reported in Table 3. Trends that were not significant are reported as 0 to be consistent with the graphs and models used. Harvest of eiders increased on average 7.5% per year during 1961-96 despite rather stable hunting regulations (Table 4). An alternative model that treated data from 1961 and 1993 as outliers and had a level shift in 1970 revealed that harvest increased 3.2% per year during 1961-96. However, we have no *a-priori* reason to include additional parameters that account for outlier points or a level shift in the model. Inspection of the lowess estimate reveals that the rate of increase probably has diminished since about 1975.

For oldsquaws and scoters, the harvest trend during 1963-71 was consistent with our hypothesis for that period, with annual rates of increase in harvest ranging from 5-17%. The trend in oldsquaw harvest during 1972-96 was also consistent with our hypothesis, showing no change. In contrast, the harvest of all scoter species declined during 1972-92, at rates ranging from 6-8% annually. The harvest of black and surf scoters during 1993-96 did not undergo the level shift decrease (i.e., drop) from the previous period that we hypothesized, whereas there was a significant drop in white-winged scoter harvest (64%) following the scoter bag limit reduction in 1993.

Availability Index.—Estimates of successful sea duck hunters were not available for 1961-64, therefore our analyses were limited to 1965-96. Availability of oldsquaw increased during both 1965-71 and 1972-96, and the rate may have diminished ($P = 0.10$), as we had hypothesized, during the later period (Fig. 10). The availability index for common eider increased on average 4.8% per year during this entire period (Fig. 10). Trends in availability indices for all three scoter species in 1972-92 were not different from those in 1965-71 (Table 5) and thus did not support our hypothesized effects of liberalized hunting seasons. Availability indices of black and surf scoters declined during 1972-92 (Table 5, Fig. 11, 12). Trends of scoter availability indices during 1993-96 were similar to those of 1972-92 (Table 5).

Index of Recruitment.—The proportion of immature birds in the harvest was highly variable for all species, but we believe that this was due more to sampling error than actual year

21

to year differences in population age structure. Sample sizes (number of wings received annually) were small for all species, averaging 75 for oldsquaw, 174 for common eider, 66 for black scoter, 148 for white-winged scoter, and 129 for surf scoter. Despite the high variability, common eider, black scoter, and surf scoter trends all suggested long-term declines in recruitment (Fig. 10-12). However, the apparent declines for black scoter and surf scoter are small compared to the variability among data points. In contrast, the lower variability in common eider age data provided stronger evidence of an actual long-term decline. Oldsquaw and white-winged scoter age structures showed little change over time (Fig. 10, 11).

Breeding Populations

Oldsquaw.—We estimate that the visibility rate of oldsquaws increased 68.71% when survey airplanes used in Alaska changed in 1977. The trend in population estimates of oldsquaw in Alaska was stable during 1957-63, then increased about 5% per year during 1964-72, and finally decreased about 6% per year after 1972 (Fig. 13). In Canada, the population was stable during 1957-63 and 1964-72, and then decreased about 6% per year in 1973-97. To determine trends for the entire Traditional Survey Area, we modeled the sum of the Alaskan series (after adjusting for change in visibility) and the Canadian series. For the Traditional Survey Area, our results were similar to those for Canada: trends during 1957-63 and 1964-72 were similar (Table 5) and stable. The population declined during 1973-97 at about 5% per year (Table 4), which was a faster decline than occurred in the previous period (Table 5). In development of our final models, we detected an approximately 65% drop in 1990 estimates from Canada and Traditional Survey Area. If these level shifts were accounted for, the rates of decline were only about 2% per year during 1973-97. We rejected these models, since we had no *a-priori* reason to hypothesize a level shift in 1990.

Nearly as many oldsquaws inhabit the Arctic Coastal Plain of Alaska as the entire Traditional Survey Area (Table 6) (King and Brackney 1997). No trend was observed in oldsquaw population estimates from the Arctic Coastal Plain during 1986-96 (King and Brackney 1997). Only a few thousand oldsquaws were found in eastern Canada and Maine during transect and plot surveys (Table 6). The combined estimates of oldsquaws from the Traditional Survey Area, the Arctic Coastal Plain, and eastern Canada and Maine averaged about 289,000 during the 1990's.

Scoters.—We estimated that the change of survey airplanes in 1977 increased the visibility of scoters 43%. Our best model of Alaskan data revealed that the number of scoters decreased at a rate of 1.7% per year during 1957-97 (Fig. 13). Our best models for the Canadian area and the Traditional Survey Area were similar, except that rate of decline was 1.6% per year in these areas. The rate of decline did not differ among periods in the Traditional Survey Area (Table 5). We evaluated 2 alternative models for the Traditional Survey Area that had different slopes for the period 1994-97. In one model the slope was increasing, and in the other model the slope was level. AIC statistics were similar for these 2 models and the one we plotted with a decreasing slope (Fig. 13). Thus, our inference on population trend during 1994-97 is equivocal. As with oldsquaws, we identified a 43% drop in 1990 in the Traditional Survey Area. Although this model had a better AIC statistic compared to the model we retained, we rejected it because we had no *a-priori* hypothesis for a level shift in 1990.

Breeding populations of scoters in eastern areas and the Arctic Coastal Plain have been smaller than those of the Traditional Survey Area during the 1990's (Table 6). On the Arctic Coastal Plain, there was no apparent trend in scoter populations during 1986-96 (King and Brackney 1997). Plot surveys in eastern Canada and Maine (Dickson 1995) indicated fewer scoters than transect surveys in a similar area. Transects surveys during the 1990's revealed around 1 million total scoters in the Traditional Survey Area, eastern areas, and the Arctic Coastal Plain (Table 6). Species composition of the scoter population is unknown on these areas. However, on plot surveys in eastern Canada and Maine, composition of the scoter population averaged about 52% surf scoters, 24% white-winged scoters, 21% black scoters, and 3% unidentified scoters (calculated from data provided in Dickson 1995).

Mid-winter Inventory

Numbers of oldsquaws on the MWI declined 1.1% per year during 1976-97 (Fig. 14). The total number of oldsquaws observed on the MWI (about 10,000) was much lower than the total observed during CBC (about 100,000) (Table 6). We detected no trend in total counts of eiders or scoters on the MWI during 1976-97 (Fig. 14). Total eider counts averaged about 104,500, while scoter counts averaged about 38,000. We detected no change in the trend of scoter counts following bag limit reductions in 1993 (Table 5).

Christmas Bird Counts

Effort adjustments.—Analysis of effort adjustments lead to a range of optimal p values, from –2.5 (all scoters) to 2.0 (black scoters). However, only common eider (p= -1.0, slope = 0.14, se(slope)=0.055) and surf scoter (p=-0.5, slope = 0.874, se(slope)=0.071) were significant. Accordingly, effort adjustments were incorporated in the analysis only for common eiders and surf scoters.

Oldsquaw.—Trends of oldsquaw based on CBC on the Atlantic Coast did not differ from zero during any interval or the entire period. Trends of CBC were not smaller during intervals with more liberal hunting regulations (Table 5).

Harlequin Duck.—We estimated trends of harlequin ducks in 2 periods, 1955-88 when hunting of harlequins was permitted in the Atlantic Flyway, and 1989-95 when no hunting was permitted. The trend was not different from zero in either period. The rate of population growth was also not significantly different between periods ($P = 0.11$). Compared to other sea ducks, relatively few harlequin ducks are observed on CBC (Table 6), and their trends should be interpreted cautiously. For example, the extreme estimate of trend (23% per year) is not significantly different from zero ($P = 0.95$), reflecting its imprecision.

Common Eider.—CBC of common eider along the Atlantic Coast during 1955-95 provided no evidence of a population trend.

Black Scoter.—Trends in CBC of black scoters along the Atlantic Coast were not different from zero during any of the intervals and during the entire period ($P > 0.9$). The trend in 1994-95, when bag limits were more restrictive, was greater than during 1973-93 (Table 5).

White-winged Scoter.—Based on CBC, the trend for white-winged scoters from 1994-95, when bag limits were restricted, was greater than in 1973-93, when regulations were most liberal ($P < 0.01$) (Table 5). Over the entire period, the trend in white-winged scoters along the Atlantic Coast was not different from zero ($P > 0.9$).

Surf Scoter.—Trends in CBC of surf scoters on the Atlantic Coast did not differ from zero in any interval, or during the entire 1955-95 period ($P < 0.9$). The trend during 1994-95, when scoter bag limits were restricted, was greater than during 1973-93, when seasons were most liberal (Table 5).

All Scoters.—No trends in total scoter CBC were detected during the entire period ($P > 0.8$) or during any interval, except possibly during 1994-95 when the trend was positive ($P = 0.06$). The trend during 1994-95 was greater than the trend during 1973-93, when regulations were most liberal (Table 5).

Sea Duck Survey

No trend was detected in counts of oldsquaws, harlequins, common eiders, or total scoters during 1991-99 (Fig. 15). Similarly, no trend was detected during 1994-99 for black scoter, white-winged scoter, and surf scoter (Fig. 15). Common eider and harlequin ducks were detected mostly in northern portions of the survey area. Harlequins were difficult to detect and only small numbers (8-54) were counted each year. Species of scoter was generally not determined during the 1991 and 1992 surveys, but beginning in 1994, species was determined for ≥85% of the scoters. The change in identification rate of scoters was due to greater emphasis on this objective and a change in survey protocol.

DISCUSSION

Limitations of Data

Bandings and Band Recoveries.—The small number of sea duck bandings and recoveries generally prohibits detailed analyses of harvest and survival rates, population affiliations, migration corridors, and other aspects of their ecology. The greatest numbers have been marked in areas where the birds are accessible and concentrated, such as at nesting colonies of eiders and white-winged scoters in southern portions of their ranges. For these birds, survival and recovery rates have been estimated (Krementz et al. 1996, Krementz et al. 1997). Although these estimates are useful, they apply only to one age-sex class and represent only a small portion of each species' range. It seems unlikely that sufficient numbers of most sea ducks could be banded and recovered in consecutive years to allow estimation of survival rates with available analytical methods. However, additional bandings and recoveries, even if from non-consecutive years, could be useful in identifying or confirming the existence of separate populations units.

Harvest, Recruitment, and Availability Indices.—Our inability to document associations between changes in regulations and changes in harvest may be due to our poor understanding of the precision of annual harvest estimates. If harvest estimates are imprecise, it is unlikely that even a strong association would be detected. This problem was magnified when we used estimates of harvest per successful sea duck hunter as an index to availability, because variance estimates for successful hunters were also unavailable. Furthermore, our use of successful sea duck hunters as a surrogate for hunter effort was based on several potentially tenuous assumptions. These assumptions include: (1) that the proportion of active sea duck hunters who were successful did not vary among years; (2) that the number of days hunted per active sea duck hunter was constant over time; and (3) that the proportion of successful sea duck hunters who were hunting specifically for sea ducks was constant over time.

Our index to recruitment, the proportion of young in the harvest, did not account for age and sex related differences in vulnerability to hunting. Differences in vulnerability can be estimated from band recovery data (Martin et al. 1979), but banding data were too limited to estimate relative vulnerability of age and sex classes of sea ducks. Another limitation of our indices of recruitment is that they are based on few samples of wings. Sampling error is greatest for those species with the smallest number of samples (i.e., oldsquaw and black scoter), and for these species we attribute much of the variation among years to sampling error.

Breeding Population.—The Breeding Waterfowl Survey appears to cover most of the scoters breeding ranges, but has 2 limitations. First, the timing of the survey usually is too early in important regions of Alaska and this may bias scoter estimates (U.S. Fish and Wildlife Service 1999). Second, species of scoters mostly have not been identified in the past, because of difficulty identifying them reliably (U.S. Fish and Wildlife Service 1999) and probably because scoters were considered less important than most other species encountered (e.g., puddle ducks) when the survey protocol was established (J. Goldsberry, U. S. Fish and Wildlife Service, personal communication). Identification of scoters to species is possible, and survey protocol in Alaska since 1998 requires this for scoters within the closest one-half of the survey transect (U.S. Fish and Wildlife Service 1999). Elsewhere in the surveyed area, protocol was modified in 1999 to allow identification of scoter species when possible. Oldsquaws can be readily identified during the Breeding Waterfowl Survey, but the survey covers only a small portion of their breeding range. Waterfowl surveys of the Arctic Coastal Plain have nearly doubled the number of oldsquaws counted compared to the Breeding Waterfowl Survey, but much of the oldsquaw breeding range still remains unsurveyed. Although identification of species of eider is feasible during low-level aerial surveys (King and Brackney 1997), this usually is not done during the Breeding Waterfowl Survey. However, even if eider species were identified, the Breeding

Waterfowl Survey still would provide only poor estimates of common eider populations, since these birds nest in coastal marine habitats that are sparsely sampled.

Mid-winter Inventory.—This survey is not based on a sampling design and provides no annual measure of precision.. It still may be a useful index to a population, if it counts a consistent proportion of that population over time. The survey probably inventories only a small proportion of sea duck populations, since it covers mostly inland and near-shore habitats (Forsell 1999). The survey has been criticized for inconsistency in survey methods, especially before 1976 (Eggeman and Johnson 1989). We believe that using data collected since 1976 minimized this potential problem. We acknowledge, however, that variation in methods still occurred and this probably affected the proportions of the total populations that were counted each year. Another limitation of this survey is that species of scoters and eiders were not distinguished. Our assumption that essentially all of the eiders counted in the Atlantic Flyway were common eiders is reasonable because other species of eiders (e.g., king eiders) are rarely seen during Christmas Bird Counts along the Atlantic Coast. Also, other species of eiders are rarely harvested in the Atlantic Flyway, even though they are legal game. The common eiders observed in the Atlantic Flyway are probably mostly American eiders, although a few northern eiders and intergrades of American and northern races undoubtedly also appear (Reed and Erskine 1986, Heusmann 1995). We have no estimate of the species composition of scoters.

Christmas Bird Counts.— This survey is primarily conducted from land areas, and probably only samples a small proportion of the habitats used by sea ducks. Sea duck habitats that are farthest offshore are very poorly represented in samples. Also, CBC tend to be concentrated near urban areas, and these areas may be over-represented in samples. Observer experience and effort varies over time and space, although effort appeared to only influence counts for 2 species. Results from the CBC may provide general information on sea duck population change, but for many species the CBC clearly does not provide precise estimates of population change.

Sea Duck Survey.—This survey has only been conducted 7 times and thus is not yet suitable for evaluation of long-term trends. Its coverage of coastal habitats is more complete than the MWI or CBC, but it too poorly represents habitats that are farther than about 0.5 miles offshore. The current extent of this survey's coverage, from Georgia to Nova Scotia, is inadequate for monitoring populations that winter farther north (e.g., king eider, northern race of the common eider) or in the Great Lakes (e.g., oldsquaws). Our analytical methods were simplified considering that data from only a few years were available. With additional data, this survey may prove to be a valuable measure of sea duck populations.

Population Status and Impacts of Hunting

The data available for managing populations of sea ducks are limited compared to many other groups of waterfowl. We have most confidence in trends that were consistent among several data sets. Trends that were found in only one measure of a species' population status should be considered cautiously.

Oldsquaw.—Indices of oldsquaw populations during 1972-96 are inconsistent; two indicated a decreasing population, one a stable population, and one an increasing population. The range in trends probably reflects the variable quality of the monitoring data. All surveys had limitations, but we believe that the CBC may be the most accurate index to oldsquaw populations wintering on the Atlantic Coast. The CBC appeals to us because of the relatively large number of oldsquaws that typically are encountered during this survey. We detected no trend in oldsquaw numbers on CBC during 1973-95. The Breeding Waterfowl Survey showed a large decrease during 1973-97, but this survey does not include eastern breeding areas and may not be reflective of oldsquaws that winter on the Atlantic Coast. We also are skeptical of results from the MWI, since this survey counts so few oldsquaws compared to the CBC.

Oldsquaw harvest increased as regulations became more liberal in the Atlantic Flyway, and stabilized when regulations remained stable. However, we found little evidence (1 or 2 cases in 5 tests) that changes in hunting regulations would lead to predictable changes in population indices.

Harlequin Duck.—Little information is available on the status of harlequin ducks in eastern North America. There are 1,000-2,000 harlequins in this area (Vickery 1988, Myers et al. 1996) and data from CBC suggest no change in trend when the hunting season was closed in the Atlantic Flyway in 1989.

Common Eider.—Population indices of common eiders reveal increasing or stable numbers in the Atlantic Flyway during 1955-97. This is consistent with a pattern of population growth that has occurred since 1907 for the eiders that nests in Maine (Krohn et al. 1992). Decreasing recruitment rates during 1961-97 may be a response to increasing densities of nesting eiders. When recruitment equals mortality, the size of the population should stabilize, assuming that immigration and emigration are negligible. Annual mortality rates for adult female American eiders in eastern North America averaged about 13% during 1977-92 (Krementz et al. 1996); mortality rates for other cohorts are unknown. We can not estimate recruitment rate without information on relative vulnerability of each age-sex class. If immatures were about 2 times as vulnerable to harvest as adults, then in 1997 about 10% of the fall population would have been immatures.

Harvest of common eiders in the Atlantic Flyway has increased despite relatively stable hunting frameworks in important harvest states and variable numbers of successful sea duck hunters across the flyway. In Maine and some other areas, guided hunts for eiders has increased during recent years (B. Allen, Maine Department of Inland Fisheries and Wildlife, personal communication), and this may at least partly account for the increasing harvest.

Black Scoter.— Overall, the black scoter population appears to be declining, but changes in regulations may affect their numerical trend. One index to their numbers during 1972-93 was decreasing, while the other index was stable. No trend was observed during 1994-96, but this inference is weak because it is based on relatively little data. Harvest in the Atlantic Flyway increased with liberalizations in regulations, but did not change when scoter bag limits were restricted in 1993. We found weak evidence from CBC that population trend changed in the direction we hypothesized when regulations were modified. Proportion of immatures in the harvest may have decreased during 1961-96.

White-winged Scoter.—The size of the white-winged scoter population appears to have been stable during 1972-93. The proportion of young in the harvest increased from low levels in the early-1980's. Hunting regulations appear to be associated with harvest and possibly population trends of white-winged scoters in the Atlantic Flyway. Harvest increased as more states selected special sea duck hunting seasons during 1963-71. Bag limit restrictions in 1993 coincided with a 64% decline in harvest of white-winged scoters and a significant increase in the trend from CBC. However, when regulations were modified at other times, trends changed in the opposite direction compared to our hypotheses.

Surf Scoter.—Numbers of surf scoters in the Atlantic Flyway may have declined during 1972-93. The proportion of immatures in the harvest also appeared to decline. Harvest of surf scoters increased when more states selected special sea duck hunting regulations during 1963-71, but did not change when bag limit of scoters were restricted in 1993. There was only weak evidence (1 case in 5 tests) that regulatory changes coincided with changes in population trends of surf scoters.

Total Scoters.—Collectively, numbers of scoters in eastern North America were either declining or stable during 1972-93. One survey, the Breeding Waterfowl Survey, indicated declining numbers, while 3 others indicated stable numbers. We consider the Breeding Waterfowl Survey to be the most reliable survey of continental scoter populations. However, it may not accurately reflect trends for scoters that winter in eastern North America. Harvest of scoters increased during 1963-71 when increasing numbers of states used Special Sea Duck Seasons. We found little evidence (1 case in 9 tests) that population trend changed in a predictable way when regulations were changed in the Atlantic Flyway.

Management Needs and Recommendations

Delineation of Populations.—Patterns of geographic distribution from breeding to wintering areas is only poorly understood for most sea ducks in North America. For example, the proportions of oldsquaw breeding in Alaska and wintering on the Pacific coast, Atlantic coast, Great Lakes, and elsewhere are unknown. Many species of sea ducks return to the same nesting area in successive years, however their propensity to return to the same wintering area is only poorly understood. Without this information, it is difficult to determine the scale at which management should be directed. Historically, harvest has been managed separately for the Atlantic and Pacific flyways in the U.S. We have implicitly adopted this strategy by analyzing data solely from the Atlantic Coast, when possible. Additional analyses of existing data (i.e. comparing population trends from different areas) may aid in determining if Atlantic and Pacific coast sea ducks share the same population dynamics, and therefore if they should be managed as one or separate populations. Additional recovery data from banded individuals would aid in this assessment. The most efficient method for assessing the amount of interchange among birds from different areas would likely utilize satellite or traditional radio telemetry techniques.

Monitoring of Population Parameters and Harvest.—Each data set that we analyzed has limitations. If population estimates were provided by species for scoters, the utility of data from the MWI and the Breeding Waterfowl Survey would increase. We recommend investigations into the feasibility of this potential improvement and implementation of consistent survey protocol across the entire area surveyed in the Breeding Waterfowl Survey area. The annual waterfowl survey of the Arctic Coastal Plain (King and Brackney 1997) appears complimentary to the Breeding Waterfowl Survey. We recommend investigations into the feasibility of integrating results from both surveys. The Sea Duck Survey warrants a more thorough review and summary than we have completed. Specifically, consideration should be given to its geographic coverage, whether sampling intensity should be modified throughout the survey area, and additional analyses that may provide more efficient estimates of population change. Regarding CBC, we encourage research to improve the efficiency of analyses and to reduce the time lag between collection of data and posting it into electronic files. We believe that the precision of harvest estimates has improved with the full implementation of the Harvest Information Program in 1998. However, estimates of the proportion of young in the harvest will still be based on relatively few samples. Managers should consider increasing the sampling intensity of successful sea duck hunters.

Harvest.—Compared to other waterfowl, sea ducks are k-strategists (Patterson 1979). They utilize relatively stable habitats, have high annual survivorship, and have low reproductive potential. Because of these characteristics, sea ducks have limited capacity to compensate for hunting mortality through increased recruitment or increased survival outside of the hunting season (Patterson 1979, Nichols et al. 1984, Krementz et al. 1996). For purposes of harvest management, we suggest that harvest mortality should be considered completely additive to natural mortality.

Our analyses demonstrated that changes in hunting regulations coincided with changes in harvest, but in only a few cases did they coincide with changes in population trends. We believe that changes in regulations can effect population growth rates, but that in most cases we were unable to detect those changes. These changes went undetected for at least 3 possible reasons: (1) variation in important environmental parameters (e.g., habitat conditions, weather) hide the minor effects of regulatory changes, (2) imprecision of surveys masked true population changes, and (3) regulatory actions outside of the Atlantic Flyway (U.S.) diluted the effects of regulatory changes within the Flyway.

The state of knowledge on sea ducks is limited compared to many other hunted waterfowl. Limitations of the data we summarized led to equivocal interpretations. Perhaps the greatest inadequacies were that total sizes of most sea duck populations have not been reliably estimated. Although sea ducks have smaller harvests than many other waterfowl, conservative hunting regulations seem prudent considering our overall state of knowledge of these birds. We recommend continued closure of hunting seasons for harlequin ducks in eastern North America unless it is demonstrated that these birds are part of a larger population. Regulations for scoters should be very conservative because of evidence of downward population trends during 1972-93, and the extreme paucity of information on black and surf scoters.

Managing the harvest of sea ducks can be contentious because some individuals and groups question the ethics of providing hunting seasons on birds that are perceived to have a high rate of non-use due to crippling and wanton waste (Federal Register 1994:42475). We recommend research to determine the contemporary rates of crippling loss, wanton waste, and hunter utilization of harvested sea ducks. We also recommend research to determine hunter preferences for bag limits and season lengths in sea duck seasons. Although this information likely would not resolve debate over the ethics of recreational hunting, it could at least eliminate speculation on the desires of hunters, and the true extent that shot ducks are utilized.

Hunting Regulations.—Two administrative issues regarding Special Sea Duck Seasons in the Atlantic Flyway warrant consideration. Specifically, these issues include: (1) is there a need to define to specific sea duck zones by Federal frameworks; and (2) do Special Sea Duck Seasons provide *additional* opportunity outside the regular duck season, or essentially the *only* opportunity for sea duck hunting? To resolve these issues, we recommend consideration of a regular sea duck season that replaces the Special Sea Duck Season, and eliminating sea ducks from the regular duck season. By doing this, sea duck season lengths and bag limits will be clearer and more specific to sea ducks, rather than confounded within seasons structured for other ducks. Regarding the need for special zones, we suggest eliminating this provision from the Federal framework. This would allow uniform seasons for sea ducks across all areas of the flyway, including inland areas on the Great Lakes. Also, those states that had specific needs for sea duck zones could define and enforce those zone restrictions through state regulations.

Management Plan and Sea Duck Joint Venture.—We recommend that the Atlantic Flyway Council in cooperation with others develop a management plan for sea ducks. The plan should not be restricted to harvest management, but should address other issues such as population monitoring, habitat management, diseases and contaminants, and information needs.

The plan should be developed in concert with the Sea Duck Joint Venture of the North American Waterfowl Management Plan.

Many information gaps impede the development of optimal harvest rates and regulations for sea ducks (Johnson et al. 1993). One deficiency is consensus on management goals for sea ducks. Development of management goals should involve managers from Canada and the U.S., and consider subsistence, recreational harvest, and non-consumptive needs. We suggest a goal to maintain populations at or above levels observed during the 1970's (U.S. Fish and Wildlife Service et al. 1994). An alternative goal might be to maintain populations at or above levels observed during recent years (1990-97).

Efforts of the proposed Sea Duck Joint Venture will not be focused solely on the Atlantic Flyway. We recommend that waterfowl managers in the Atlantic Flyway Council fully participate in joint venture activities, so as to insure that their regional needs are addressed while also promoting coordinated management and strategic research. The proposed Sea Duck Joint Venture can also serve to improve communications among researchers and managers, and aid in the administration of research and management activities.

LITERATURE CITED

Abraham, K. F., and G. H. Finney. 1986. Eiders of the eastern Canadian arctic. Pages 55-73 *in* A. Reed, editor, Eider ducks in Canada. Canadian Wildlife Service Report Series 47.

Ad Hoc Sea Duck Committee Atlantic Flyway Technical Section. 1994. Status of sea ducks in the Atlantic Flyway with strategies towards improved management. Unpublished report, Technical Section Atlantic Flyway Council.

Alison, R. M. 1975. Breeding biology and behavior of the oldsquaw (*Clangula hyemalis* L.). Ornithological Monographs 18.

Barry, G. J., P. L. Flint, R. F. Rockwell, M. R. Petersen, and T. L. Moran. 1997. Population dynamics of spectactled eiders on Yukon-Kuskokwim Delta, Alaska (abstract only). Page 23 *in* Proceedings First North America Duck Symposium and Workshop, Baton Rouge, Louisiana, USA.

Bellrose, F. C. 1980. Ducks, geese and swans of North America. Third edition Stackpole Books, Harrisburg, Pennsylvania, USA.

Bengtson, S. 1965. Field studies on the harlequin duck in Iceland. Wildfowl Trust Annual Report 17:79-94.

Bent, A. C. 1925. Life histories of North American wild fowl (part II). U.S. Natural Museum Bulletin 130, Washington, D.C., USA.

Bordage, D., and J. L. Savard. 1995. Black scoter. Birds of North America 177.

Box, G.E.P., and G. M. Jenkins. 1970. Time series analysis: forecasting and control. Holden-Day, San Francisco, USA.

Brandt, H. 1943. Alaska bird trails: an expedition by dog sled to the delta of the Yukon River at Hooper Bay. The Bird Research Foundation, Cleveland, Ohio, USA.

Brown, P. W., and C. S. Houston. 1982. Longevity and age of maturity of white-winged scoters. Journal Field Ornithology 53:53-54.

_____, and L. H. Fredrickson. 1986. Food habits of breeding white-winged scoters. Canadian Journal of Zoology 64:1652-1654.

_____, _____. 1989. White-winged scoter, *Melanitta fusca*, populations and nesting on Redberry Lake, Saskatchewan. Canadian Field-Naturalist 103:240-247.

_____, and _____. 1997. White-winged scoter. Birds of North America 274.

_____, and M. A. Brown. 1981. Nesting biology of the white-winged scoter. Journal of Wildlife Management 45:38-45.

Butcher, G. S. 1990. The Audubon Christmas Bird Count. Pages 5-13 *in* J. R. Sauer and S. Droege, editors. Survey designs and statistical methods for the estimation of avian population trends. U. S. Fish and Wildlife Service Biological Report 90(1).

Canadian Wildlife Service and U.S. Fish and Wildlife Service. 1987. Standard Operation Procedures for aerial waterfowl breeding ground population and habitat surveys in North America, unpublished report, U.S. Fish and Wildlife Service, Arlington, Virginia, USA.

_____, _____, and U.S. Geological Survey. 1997. Conservation issues for North American sea ducks. 27 November draft of unpublished report.

Carney, S. M. 1992. Species, age and sex identification of ducks using wing plumage. U.S. Fish and Wildlife Service, Washington, D. C., USA.

Carroll, R.J. and D. Ruppert. 1988. Transformation and weighting in regression. Chapman & Hall , New York, New York, USA.

Cassirer, E. F., C. R. Groves, and R. L. Wallen. 1991. Distribution and population status of harlequin ducks in Idaho. Wilson Bulletin 103:723-725.

Cleveland, W.S. 1979. Robust locally weighted regression and smoothing scatterplots. Journal of American Statistical Association 79:368, 829-836.

Conroy, M. J., J. R. Goldsberry, J. E. Hines, and D. B. Stotts. 1988. Evaluation of aerial transect surveys for wintering American black ducks. Journal of Wildlife Management 52:694-703.

Cooch, F. G. 1965. The breeding biology and management of the northern eider (*Somateria mollissima borealis*) in the Cape Dorset area, Northwest Territories. Canadian Wildlife Service Wildlife Management Bulletin (Series 2) 10.

Cooch, F. G., S. Wendt, G. E. J. Smith, and G. Butler. 1978. The Canadian Migratory Game Bird Hunting Permit and associated surveys. Pages 8-39 *in* H. Boyd and G. H. Finney, editors. Migratory game bird hunters and hunting in Canada. Canadian Wildlife Service Report Series 43.

Cottam, C. 1939. Food habits of North American diving ducks. U.S. Department of Agriculture Technical Bulletin 643.

Dickson, K. 1995. Breeding waterfowl survey in Eastern Canada and the state of Maine. Canadian Wildlife Service unpublished report.

Di Giulio, R. T., and P. F. Scanlon. 1984. Heavy metals in tissues of waterfowl from the Chesapeake Bay, USA. Environmental Pollution Series A35:29-48.

Draper, N. and H. Smith. 1981. Applied regression analysis. Second edition. John Wiley & Sons, New York, New York, USA.

Dunn, E. H., and J. R. Sauer. 1997. Monitoring Canadian bird populations with winter counts. Pages 49-55 *in* Dunn, E. H., M. D. Cadman, and J. Bruce Falls, editors, Monitoring bird populations: the Canadian experience. Canadian Wildlife Service, Occasional Paper 95.

Eggeman, D. R., and F. A. Johnson. 1989. Variation in effort and methodology for the midwinter waterfowl inventory in the Atlantic Flyway. Wildlife Society Bulletin 17:227-233.

Federal Register. 1994. 50 CFR Part 20 Migratory bird hunting; final frameworks for early-season migratory bird hunting regulations; final rule. 59(158):42475.

Forsell, D. J. 1999. Distribution and abundance of sea ducks wintering in Chesapeake Bay. Page 81 *in* Goudie, R. I., M. R. Petersen, and G. J. Robertson, editors, Behaviour and ecology of sea ducks. Canadian Wildlife Service, Occasional Paper 100.

Franson, J. C., M. R. Petersen, C. U. Meteyer, and M. R. Smith. 1995. Lead poisoning of spectacled eiders (*Somateria fischeri*) and of a common eider (*Somateria mollissima*) in Alaska. Journal of Wildlife Disease 31:268-271.

Geissler, P. H. 1990. Estimation of confidence intervals for federal waterfowl harvest surveys. Journal of Wildlife Management 54:201-205.

_____, and J. R. Sauer. 1990. Topics in route regression analysis. Pgs 54-57 *in* J. R. Sauer and S. Droege, eds. Survey designs and statistical methods for the estimation of avian population trends. U. S. Fish and Wildlife Service, Biological Report 90(1).

R. I. Goudie. 1989. Historical status of harlequin ducks wintering in eastern North America—a reappraisal. Wilson Bulletin 101:112-114.

Goudie, R. I., A. V. Kondratyev, S. Brault, M. R. Petersen, B. Conant, K. Vermeer. 1994. The status of sea ducks in the North Pacific Rim: toward their conservation and management. Transactions North American Wildlife Natural Resource Conference 59:27-45.

Hochbaum, H. A. 1944. The canvasback on a prairie marsh. American Wildlife Institute, Washington, D. C., USA.

Hodges, J. I., J. G. King, B. Conant, and H. A. Hanson. 1996. Aerial surveys of waterbirds in Alaska 1957-94: Population trends and observer variability. Information Technology Report 4. National Biological Service, U.S. Department of Interior, Washington, D. C., USA.

Hohman, W. L., C. D. Ankney, and D. H. Gordon. 1992. Ecology and management of postbreeding waterfowl. Pages 128-189 *in* B. D. J. Batt, A. D. Afton, M. G. Anderson, C. D. Ankney, D. H. Johnson, J. A. Kadlec, and G. L. Krapu, editors. Ecology and management of breeding waterfowl. University of Minnesota Press, Minneapolis, Minnesota, USA.

Heusmann, H W. 1995. The eider duck. Massachusetts Wildlife 45(1):31-37.

Hurvich, C. M., and C. Tsai. 1989. Regression and time series model selection in small samples. Biometrika 76:297–307.

Jarvis, R. L., and H. Bruner. 1996. Characterization of habitat used by breeding harlequin ducks in Oregon. Oregon State University unpublished Progress Report, Corvailles, Oregon, USA.

Johnsgard, P. A. 1975. Waterfowl of North America. Indiana University Press, Bloomington, Indiana, USA.

_____. 1978. Ducks, geese, and swans of the world. University of Nebraska Press, Lincoln, Nebraska, USA.

Johnson, F. A., B. K. Williams, J. D. Nichols, J. E. Hines, W. L. Kendall, G. W. Smith, and D. F. Caithamer. 1993. Developing an adaptive management strategy for harvesting waterfowl in North America. Transactions North American Wildlife and Natural Resource Conference 58:565-583.

Johnson, S. R., and W. J. Richardson. 1982. Waterbird migration near the Yukon and Alaskan coast of the Beaufort Sea: 2. Moult migration of seaducks in summer. Arctic 35:291-301.

Johnstone, S. T. 1970. Waterfowl eggs. Avicultural Magazine 76:52-55.

Kehoe, F. P. 1989. The adaptive significance of crèching behaviour in the white-winged scoter (*Melanitta fusca deglandi*). Canadian Journal of Zoology 67:406-411.

Kertell, K. 1991. Disappearance of the Steller's eider from the Yukon-Kuskokwim Delta, Alaska. Arctic 44:177-187.

King, R. J., and A. W. Brackney. 1997. Aerial breeding pair surveys of the Arctic Coastal Plain of Alaska – 1996. Unpublished report, U.S. Fish and Wildlife Service, Anchorage, Alaska, USA.

Korschgen, C. E. 1977. Breeding stress of female eiders in Maine. Journal of Wildlife Management 41:360-373.

Krementz, D. G., J. E. Hines, and D. F. Caithamer. 1996. Survival and recovery rates of American eiders in eastern North America. Journal of Wildlife Management 60:855-862.

_____, P. W. Brown, F. P. Kehoe, and C. S. Houston. 1997. Population dynamics of white-winged scoters. Journal of Wildlife Management 61:222-227.

Krohn, W. B., P. O. Corr, and A. E. Hutchinson. 1992. Status of the American eider with special reference to northern New England. U.S. Fish and Wildlife Report. 12.

Link, W. A., and J. R. Sauer. 1994. Estimating equations estimates of trends. Bird Populations 2:23-32.

_____, and _____. 1999. Controlling for varying effort in count surveys – an analysis of Christmas Bird Count data. Journal of Agricultural, Biological, and Environmental Statistics 4:116-125.

Martin, E. M., and S. M. Carney. 1977. Population ecology of the mallard part IV. A review of duck hunting regulations, activity, and success, with special reference to the mallard. Resource Publication 130, U.S. Fish and Wildlife Service, Washington, D.C., USA.

_____, and P. I. Padding. 1997. Preliminary estimates of waterfowl harvest and hunter activity in the United States during the 1996 hunting season. U.S. Fish and Wildlife Service, Laurel, Maryland, USA.

Martin, F. W., R. S. Pospahala, and J. D. Nichols. 1979. Assessment and population management of North American migratory birds. Pages 187-239 in J. Cairns, Jr., G. P. Patil, and W. E. Waters, editors Environmental biomonitoring, assessment, prediction, and management – certain case studies and related quantitative issues. Statistical Ecology, Volume 11. International Cooperative Publication House, Fairland, Maryland, USA.

Mawhinney, K., and A. W. Diamond. 1997. Status of the common eider (*Somateria mollissima*) in New Brunswick (abstract only). Page 26 in Proceedings of First North America Duck Symposium and Workshop, Baton Rouge, Louisiana, USA.

Mendall, H. L. 1968. An inventory of Maine's breeding eider ducks. Transactions Northeastern Section Wildlife Society Conference 25:95-104.

Mendenhall, V. M., and H. Milne. 1985. Factors affecting duckling survival of eiders Somateria mollissima in northeast Scotland. Ibis 127:148-158.

Mielke, P. W., K. J. Berry, P. J. Brockwell, and J. S. Williams. 1981. A class of nonparametric tests based on multiresponse permutation procedures. Biometrica 68:720-724.

Montalbano, F., III, F. A. Johnson, and M. J. Conroy. 1985. Status of wintering ring-necked ducks in the southern Atlantic Flyway. Journal of Wildlife Management 49:543-546.

Munro, J., and J. Bédard. 1977. Crèche formation in the common eider. Auk 94:759-771.

Myers, J. E., G. H. Haas, and P. Kehoe. 1996. Population status of harlequin ducks in the north Atlantic region. Unpublished report, Rhode Island Division of Fish and Wildlife, West Kingston, Rhode Island, USA.

Nichols, J. D., M. J. Conroy, D. R. Anderson, and K. P. Burnham. 1984. Compensatory mortality in waterfowl populations: a review of the evidence and implications for research and management. Transactions North American Wildlife and Natural Resource Conferance 54:535-554.

Ohlendorf, H. M., R. W. Olwe, P. R. Kelly, and T. E. Harvey. 1986. Selenium and heavy metals in San Francisco Bay diving ducks. Journal of Wildlife Management 50:64-71.

_____, and W. J. Fleming. 1988. Birds and environmental contaminants in San Francisco and Chesapeake bays. Marine Pollution Bulletin 19:487-495.

Office of Migratory Bird Management. 1993. Status of sea ducks in eastern North America. U.S. Fish and Wildlife Service unpublished report, Laurel, Maryland, USA.

Oring, L. W., and R. D. Sayler. 1992. The mating systems of waterfowl. Pages 190-213 *in* B. D. J. Batt, A. D. Afton, M. G. Anderson, C. D. Ankney, D. H. Johnson, J. A. Kadlec, and G. L. Krapu, editors. Ecology and management of breeding waterfowl. University of Minnesota Press, Minneapolis, Minnesota, USA.

Patterson, J. H. 1979. Can ducks be managed by regulation? Transactions North American Wildlife and Natural Resources Conferance 44:130-139.

Piatt, J. F., C. J. Lensink, W. Butler, M. Kendziorek, and D. R. Nysewander. 1990. Immediate impact of the 'Exxon Valdez' oil spill on marine birds. Auk 107:387-397.

Prach, R. W., A. R. Smith, and A. Dzubin. 1986. Nesting of the common eider near the Hell Gate – Cardigan Strait polynya, 1980-81. Pages 127-135 *in* A. Reed, editor, Eider ducks in Canada. Canadian Wildlife Service Report Series 47.

Reed, A., and A. J. Erskine. 1986. Populations of the common eider in eastern North America: their size and status. Pages 156-162 *in* A. Reed, editor, Eider ducks in Canada. Canadian Wildlife Service Report Series 47.

_____, Y. Aubry, and E. Reed. 1994. Surf scoter, *Melanitta perspicillata*, nesting in southern Quebec. Canadian Field-Naturalist 108:364-365.

Salomonsen, F. 1968. The moult migration. Wildfowl 19:5-24.

Salter, R., M. A. Gollop, S. R. Johnson, W. R. Koski, and C. E. Tull. 1980. Distribution and abundance of birds on the Arctic Coastal Plain of northern Yukon and adjacent Northwest Territories. Canadian Field-Naturalist 94:219-238.

Sauer, J. R., and J. B. Bortner. 1991. Population trends from the American woodcock singing-ground survey, 1970-88. Journal of Wildlife Management 55:300-312.

_____, and P. H. Geissler. 1990. Annual indices from route regression analyses. Pgs 58-62 *in* J. R. Sauer and S. Droege, editors. Survey designs and statistical methods for the estimation of avian population trends. U. S. Fish and Wildlife Service, Biological Report 90(1).

_____, S. Schwartz, and B. Hoover. 1996. The Christmas Bird Count Home Page (http://www.mbr.nbs.gov/bbs/cbc.html). Version 95.1. Patuxent Wildlife Research Center, Laurel, Maryland, USA.

Savard, J. L., and P. Lamothe. 1991. Distribution, abundance, and aspects of breeding ecology of black scoters, *Melanitta nigra*, and surf scoters, *M. perspicillata*, in northern Quebec. Canadian Field-Naturalist 105:489-496.

Sibley, C. G., and B. L. Monroe, Jr. 1990. Distribution and taxonomy of birds of the world. Yale University Press, New Haven, Connecticut, USA.

Slauson, W. L., B. S. Cade, and J. D. Richards. 1991. User manual for BLOSSOM statistical software. National Ecological Research Center, U.S. Fish and Wildlife Service, Fort Collins, Colorado, USA.

Smith, G. W. 1995. A critical review of the aerial and ground surveys of breeding waterfowl in North America. National Biological Service, Biological Science Report 5.

Spurr, E., and H. Milne. 1976. Adaptive significance of autumn pair formation in the common eider *Somateria mollissima* (L.). Ornis Scandinavica 7:85-89.

Stehn, R. A., C. P. Dau, B. Conant, and W. I. Butler. 1993. Decline of spectacled eiders nesting in western Alaska. Arctic 46: 264-277.

Stott, R. S., and D. P. Olson. 1973. Food-habitat relationships of sea ducks on the New Hampshire coastline. Ecology 54:996-1007.

Stotts, V. D. 1966. Observation of waterfowl in deep-water areas from mid-October to mid-January, 1965-66. Unpublished report, Maryland Department of Game and Inland Fisheries, Annapolis, Maryland, USA.

Time Series Staff of Census Bureau Statistical Research Division. 1995. REGARIMA reference manual on the Census Bureau Home Page (http:/www.Census.Gov/pub/ts/regarima). Washington, D. C., USA.

U.S. Fish and Wildlife Service. 1988. Supplemental environmental impact statement: issuance of annual regulations permitting the sport hunting of migratory birds. U.S. Department of Interior, Washington, D. C., USA.

_____. 1999. Population status and trends of sea ducks in Alaska. Unpublished report, Migratory Bird Management, Waterfowl Management Branch, Anchorage, Alaska, USA.

_____, Environment Canada, and Desarrollo Social Mexico. 1994. 1994 Update to the North American Waterfowl Management Plan. U.S. Fish and Wildlife Service, Washington, D.C.

Van Dijk, B. 1986. The breeding biology of eiders at Ile aux Pommes, Quebec. Pages 119-126 *in* A. Reed, editor, Eider ducks in Canada. Canadian Wildlife Service Report Series 47.

Vickery, P. D. 1988. Distribution and population status of Harlequin ducks (*Histrionicus histrionicus*) wintering in eastern North America. Wilson Bulletin 100:119-126.

Table 1. Periods of sea duck hunting regulations in the Atlantic Flyway (U. S.) and hypotheses (alternative) of period-effects on harvests and populations indices of oldsquaws and scoters.

	Period				
	1955-62[1]	1963-71[2]	1972-96[3]	1972-92[4]	1993-96[5]
Regulations	Stable and conservative	Increasing number of states use special sea duck seasons	Stable and liberal	Stable and liberal, bag limits for scoters = 7	Stable, bag limits for scoters = 4
Hypothesized effects on oldsquaws					
Harvest	Not evaluated	Increasing	Stable		
Index of availability	Not evaluated	Lower rate of growth than in previous period	Lower rate of growth than in previous period		
Breeding Population	Stable	Lower rate of growth than in previous period	Lower rate of growth than in previous period		
Mid-winter Index	No data	No data	Stable		
Christmas Bird Count	Stable	Lower rate of growth than in previous period	Lower rate of growth than in previous period		
Hypothesized effects on scoters					
Harvest	Not evaluated	Increasing		Stable	Stable, but at lower level than previous period
Index of availability	Not evaluated	Lower rate of growth than in previous period		Lower rate of growth than in previous period	Greater rate of growth than in previous period
Breeding Population	Stable	Lower rate of growth than in previous period		Lower rate of growth than in previous period	Greater rate of growth than in previous period
Mid-winter Index	No data	No data		Stable	Greater rate of growth than in previous period
Christmas Bird Count	Stable	Lower rate of growth than in previous period		Lower rate of growth than in previous period	Greater rate of growth than in previous period

[1] Periods used were 1957-63 for breeding population estimates and 1955-63 for Christmas Bird Counts (CBC's).
[2] Periods used were 1965-71 for availability indices, and 1964-72 for breeding population estimates and CBC's.
[3] Periods used were 1973-97 for breeding population estimates and CBC's, and 1976-97 for mid-winter indices.
[4] Periods used were 1973-93 for breeding population estimates and CBC's, and 1976-93 for mid-winter indices.
[5] Periods used were 1994-97 for breeding population estimates and CBC's, and 1994-97 for mid-winter indices.

Table 2. Total numbers of bandings and band recoveries of select species of sea ducks in North America. Data were retrieved in September 1997 from records of the Bird Banding Laboratory, U.S. Geological Survey, Laurel, Maryland.

	Banded	Recovered
Oldsquaw	2569	58
Harlequin	3765	231
Common eider	20425	2747
Black scoter	114	4
White-winged scoter	2950	136
Surf scoter	395	14

Table 3. Estimated changes in harvests of sea ducks in the Atlantic Flyway (U.S.) during different regulatory periods, 1963-96.

	Regulatory period					
	1963-71		1972-92(6)[1]		1993-96[2]	
Species	Slope (% change/year)	P (slope coeff ≤ 0)	Slope (% change/year)	P (slope coeff ≠ 0)	Level shift(%) from previous period	P (level shift ≥ 0)
Oldsquaw	17	<0.001	0	>0.05		
Black scoter	13	<0.001	-8	<0.001	0	>0.05
White-winged scoter	5	0.02	-6	0.001	-64	0.002
Surf scoter	13	<0.001	-7	<0.001	0	>0.05
All scoters	11	<0.001	-8	<0.001	0	>0.05

[1]Periods used were 1972-92 for scoters and 1972-96 for oldsquaws.

[2]Level shifts estimated for scoters only.

Table 4. Rates of changes (percent annual changes) in harvest and population estimates of sea ducks, during recent time periods. Breeding population estimates and mid-winter counts were not available for individual species of scoters or eiders. Time periods evaluated vary due to limitations in data and variations in hypotheses.

Estimate and region	Oldsquaw		Common eider[1]		Black scoter		White-winged scoter		Surf scoter		All scoters	
	Rate	Period	Rate	Period	Rate	Period	Rate	Period	Rate	Period	Rate	Period
Harvest estimates for Atlantic Flyway	NS[2]	1972-96	7.5	1961-96	-4.1	1972-92	-3.2	1972-92	-3.7	1972-92	-4.2	1972-92
Availability index for Atlantic Flyway	2.8	1972-96	4.8	1965-96	-1.9	1972-92	NS	1972-92	-1.7	1972-92	NS	1972-92
Breeding population estimates of traditional survey area[3]	-5.3	1973-97									-1.6	1973-93
Mid-winter Inventories of Atlantic Flyway	-1.1	1976-97	NS	1976-97							NS	1976-93
Christmas Bird Counts from Atlantic Coast	NS	1973-95	NS	1955-95	NS	1973-93	NS	1973-93	NS	1973-93	NS	1973-93

[1] Mid-winter inventory includes all species of eiders.

[2] Not significantly different (P>0.05) from zero.

[3] The traditional survey area is strata 1-50 and 75-77.

Table 5. Comparisons, between regulation periods, of rates of change in population estimates of sea ducks. Periods for breeding population estimates, mid-winter inventories, and Christmas Bird Counts lag one year behind those of availability indices.

| | | Regulatory periods compared | | | | | |
| | | 1955-62[1] vs 1963-71[2] | | 1963-71[2] vs 1972-92(6)[3] | | 1972-92[3] vs 1993-96[4] | |
Species	Estimate[5]	d[6]	$P(d \geq 0)$	d	$P(d \geq 0)$	d	$P(d \leq 0)$
Oldsquaw	Availability index	NC[7]		-6	0.10	NC	
	Breeding population estimate	4	0.78	-6	<0.01	NC	
	Christmas Bird Count	-10	0.39	-12	0.33	NC	
Black scoter	Availability index	NC		-1	0.13	2	0.44
	Christmas Bird Count	13	0.36	-11	0.32	28	<0.01
White-winged scoter	Availability index	NC		9	0.98	8	0.25
	Christmas Bird Count	-19	0.23	-21	0.11	47	<0.01
Surf scoter	Availability index	NC		3	0.72	-2	0.55
	Christmas Bird Count	-1	0.48	-11	0.24	69	<0.01
All scoters	Availability index	NC		6	0.96	2	0.42
	Breeding population estimate	-3	0.13	3	0.94	-5	0.87
	Mid-winter inventory	NC		NC		4	0.12
	Christmas Bird Count	12	0.25	-4	0.35	348	<0.01

[1]Periods used were 1957-63 for breeding population estimates and 1955-63 for Christmas Bird Counts.

[2]Periods used were 1965-71 for availability indices, and 1964-72 for breeding population estimates and Christmas Bird Counts.

[3]Periods used were 1972-93 for scoter availability indices; 1972-96 for oldsquaw availability indices; 1973-97 for oldsquaw breeding populations; 1976-97 for oldsquaw mid-winter inventories; 1973-93 for scoter breeding populations and Christmas Bird Counts; and 1976-93 for scoter mid-winter inventories.

[4]Periods used were 1994-97 for scoter breeding populations and mid-winter inventories, and 1994-95 for scoter Christmas Bird Counts.

[5]Availability index and mid-winter inventory were from the Atlantic Flyway, breeding population estimate was from the Traditional Survey Area, and Christmas Bird Count was from the Atlantic coast.

[6](slope coefficient of second period)-(slope coefficient of first period); positive number means that slope coefficient is larger in the second period.

[7]No comparison was possible.

Table 6. Means of selected sea duck population indices (thousands) in North America during the 1990's.

Survey and region	Years	Oldsquaw	Harlequin duck	Common eider	All eiders	Black scoter	White-winged scoter	Surf scoter	All scoters
Breeding Population Survey of Traditional Area (strata 1-50, 75-77)	1990-97	169.9			9.0				953.1
Breeding Population Survey of Eastern Area (strata 51-68)[1]	1990-97	3.1			112.4				68.1
Breeding Population Survey of Arctic Coastal Plain[2]	1990-96	116.4		1.9	19.5				12.9
Breeding Population Survey of all areas[1]	1990-97	289.4		1.9	140.9				1034.1
Eastern Plot Survey of breeding populations[3]	1990-95	3.1	0.1	6.2		4.8	5.5	12.2	23.2
Mid-winter Inventory of Atlantic Flyway	1990-97	10.7			133.8				56.4
Sea Duck Survey of Atlantic Coast	1991-97	8.9	<0.1	33.1		8.3[4]	3.1[4]	10.3[4]	25.7
Christmas Bird Count of Atlantic Coast	1990-95	111.5	0.1	70.3		6.6	27.3	11.5	58.4

[1] All strata not surveyed in each year.
[2] Data from King and Brackney (1997).
[3] Data from Dickson (1995).
[4] Means from years 1994, 1995, and 1997-99 only.

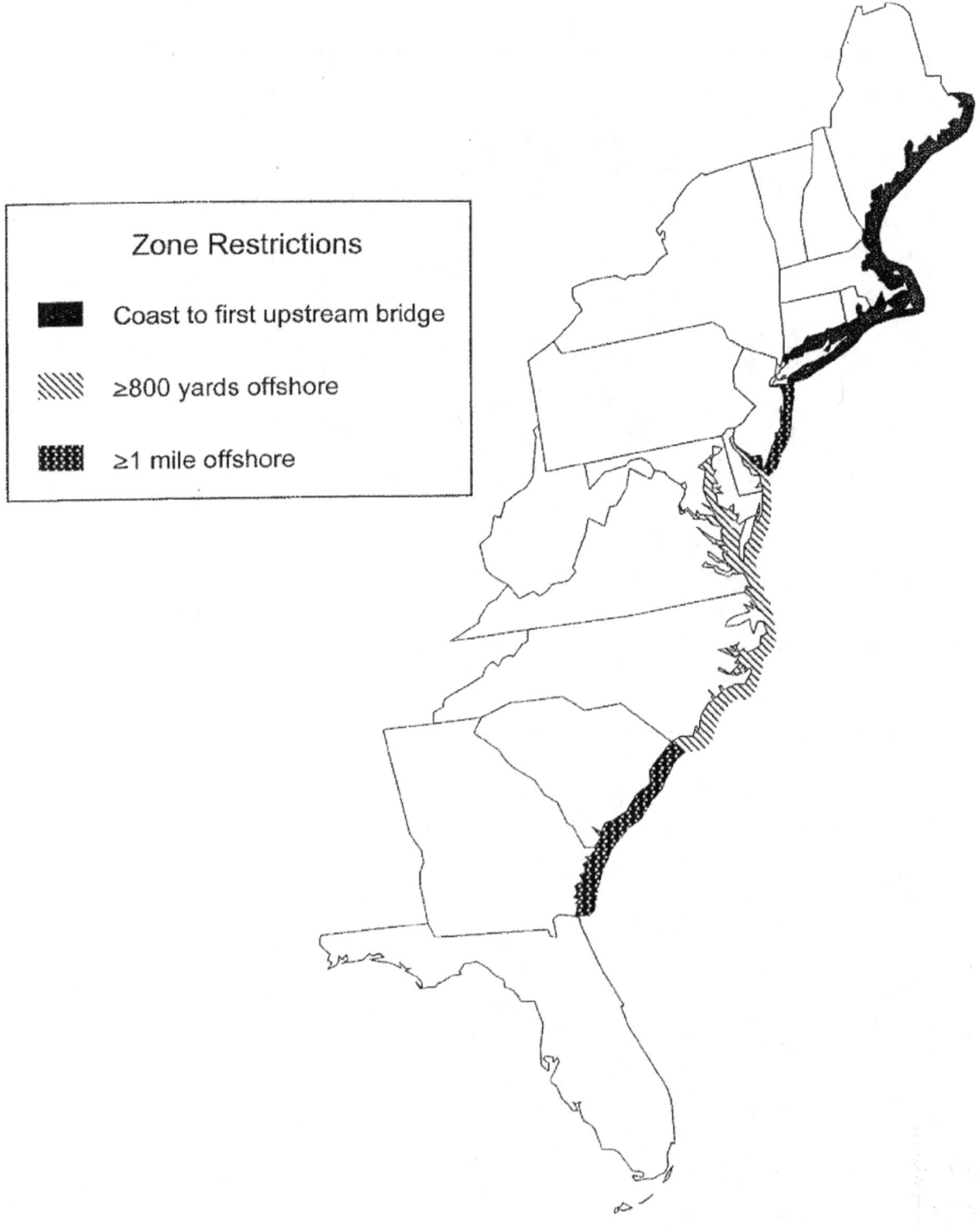

Fig. 1. Special sea duck hunting zones in the Atlantic Flyway during the 1997-98 hunting season.

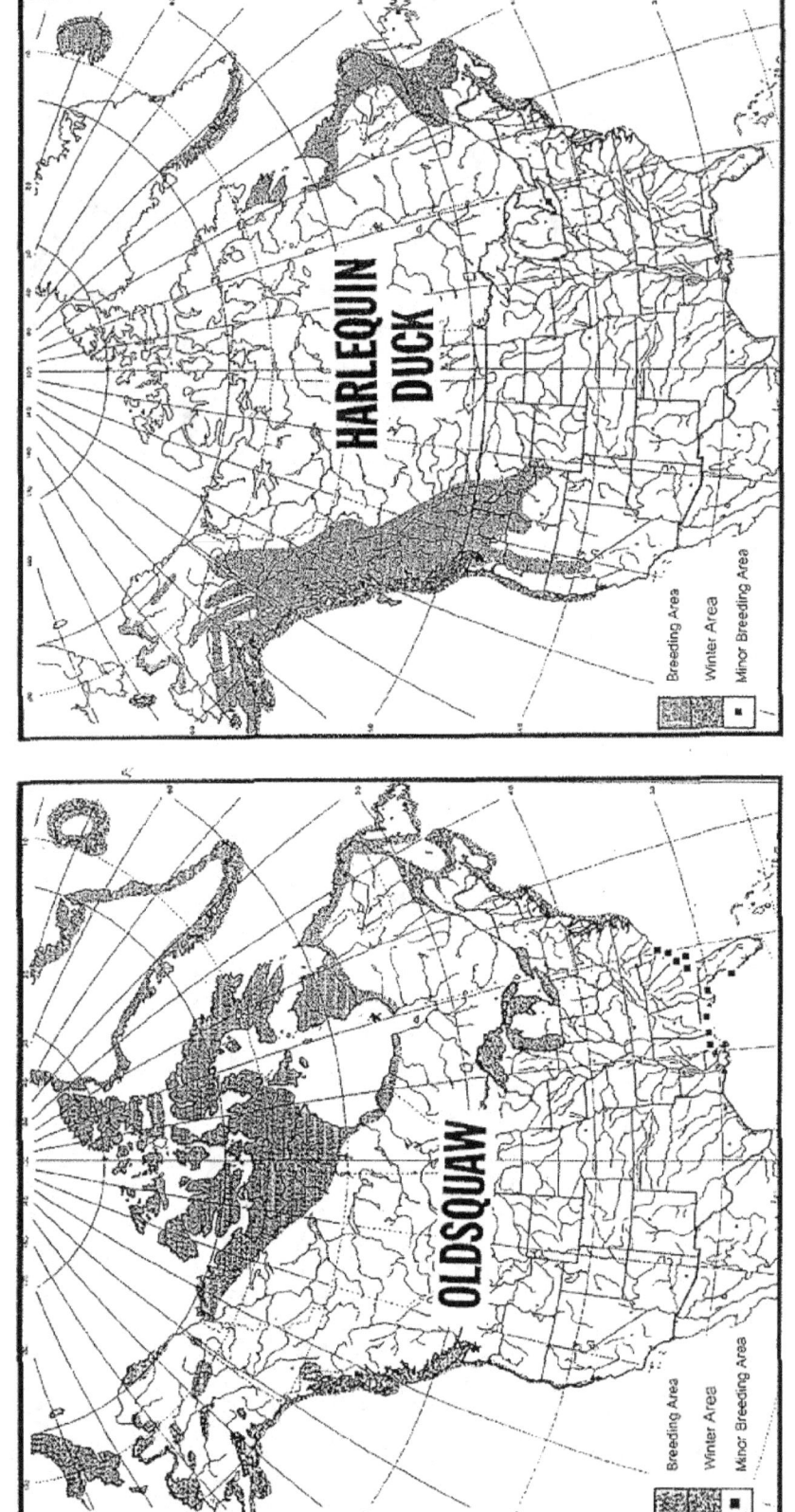

Fig. 2. Distribution of oldsquaw and harlequin ducks in North America (from Bellrose 1980). Reproduced with permission of Wildlife Management Institute.

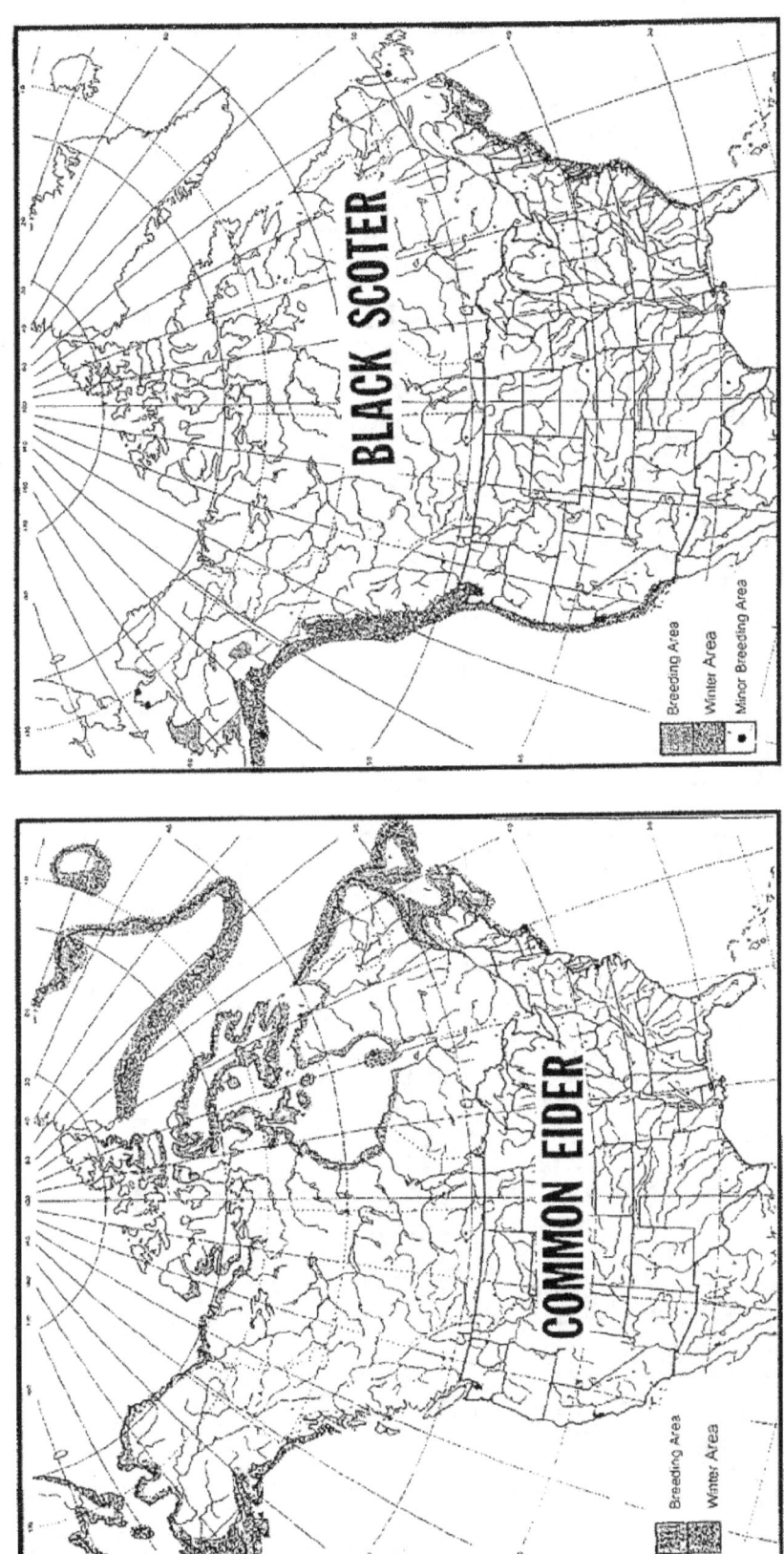

Fig. 3. Distribution of common eider and black scoter in North America (from Bellrose 1980). Reproduced with permission of Wildlife Management Institute.

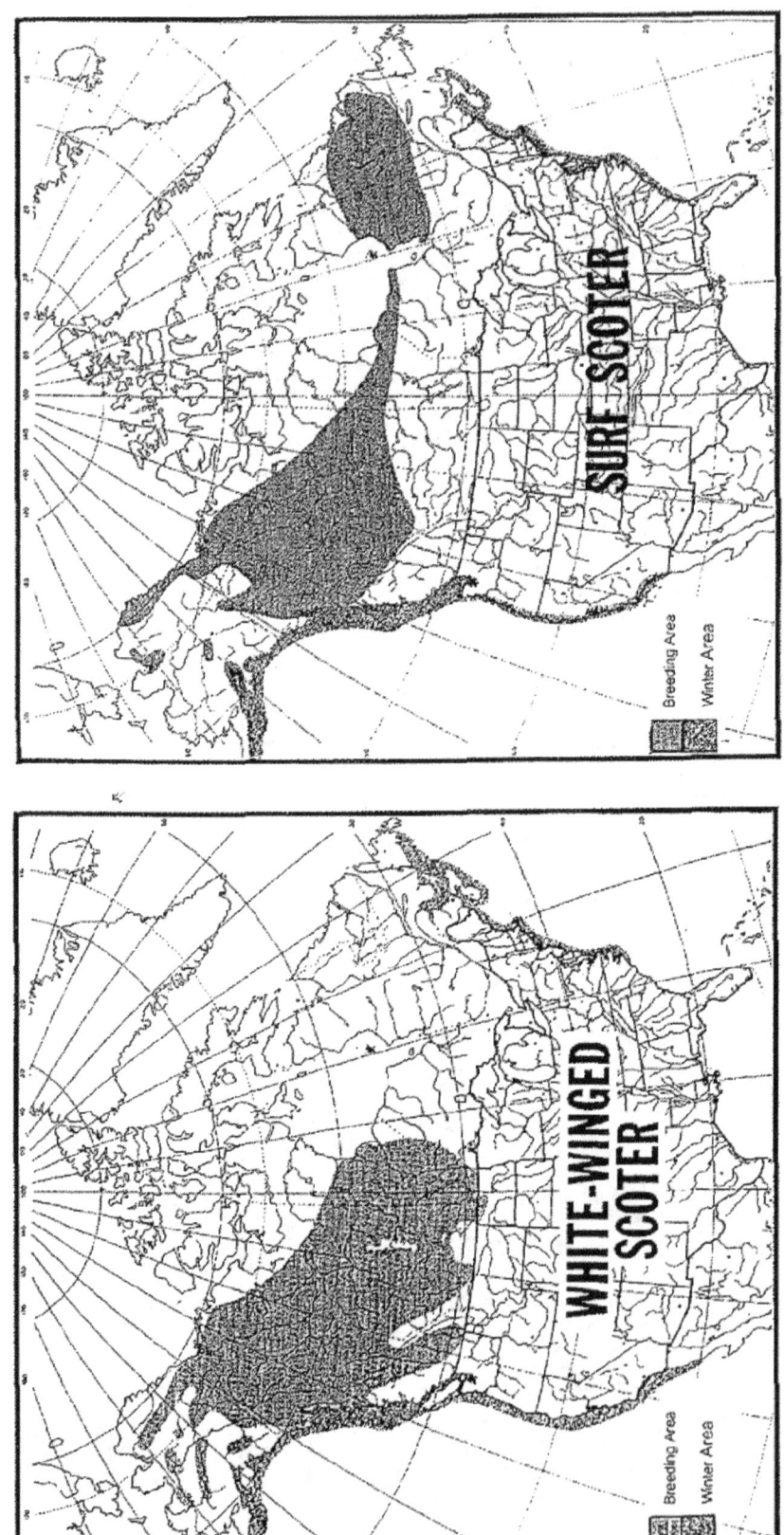

Fig. 4. Distribution of white-winged and surf scoters in North America (from Bellrose 1980). Reproduced with permission of Wildlife Management Institute.

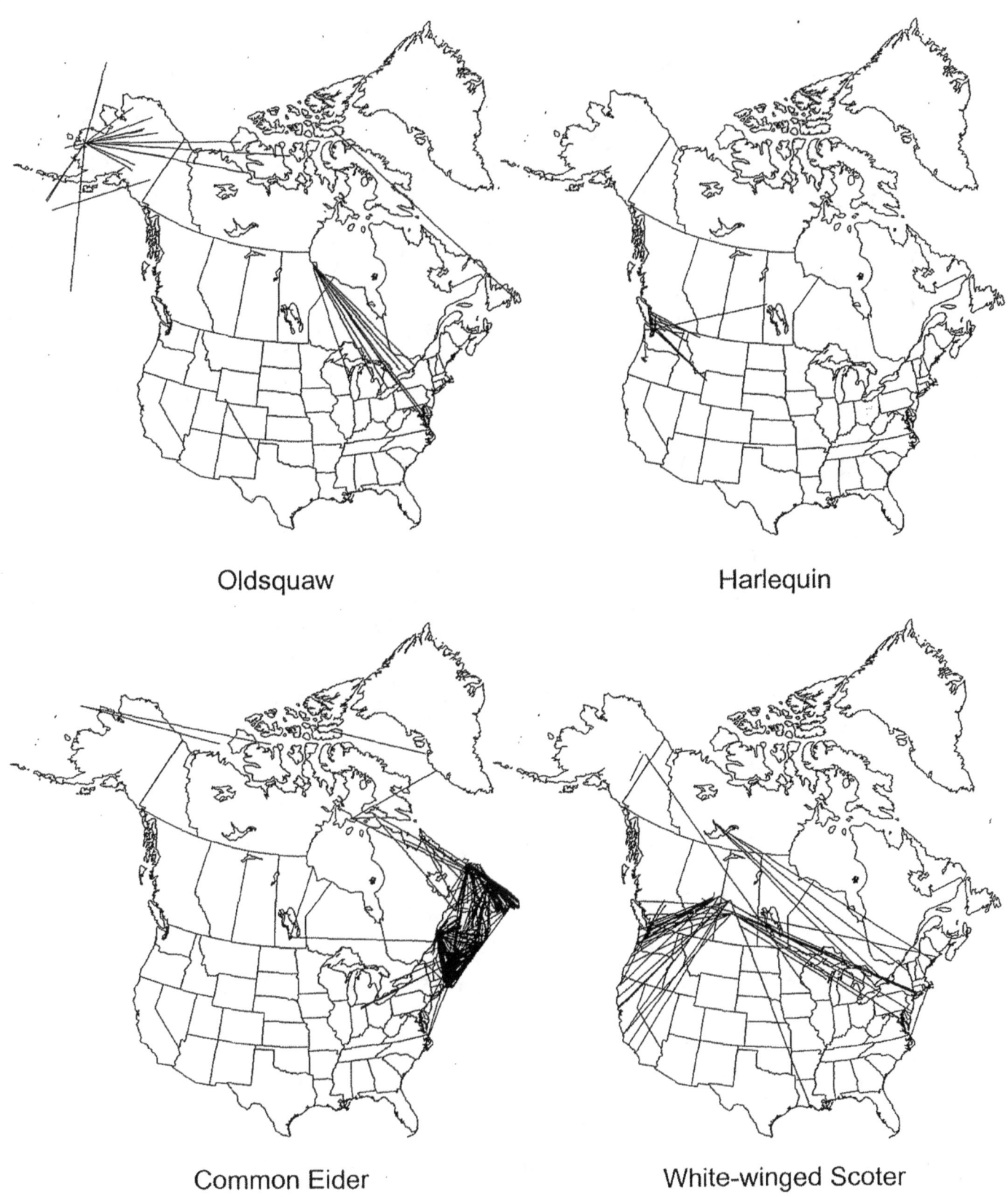

Oldsquaw

Harlequin

Common Eider

White-winged Scoter

Fig. 5. Banding and recovery locations (connected with a line) of all bands recovered from selected species of sea ducks. No line is shown where the banding location was the same as the recovery location. Data were obtained in September 1997.

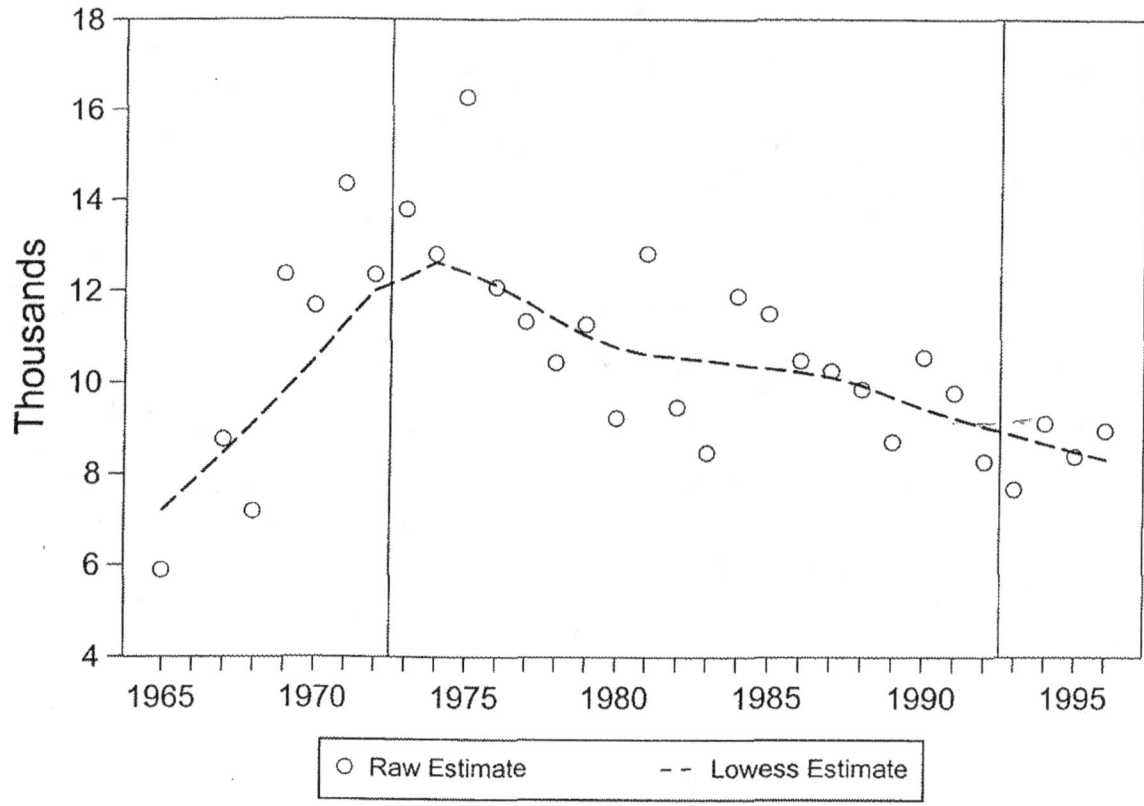

Fig. 6. Estimated numbers of successful sea duck hunters in the Atlantic Flyway, 1965-96. Vertical lines mark periods with major differences in hunting regulations.

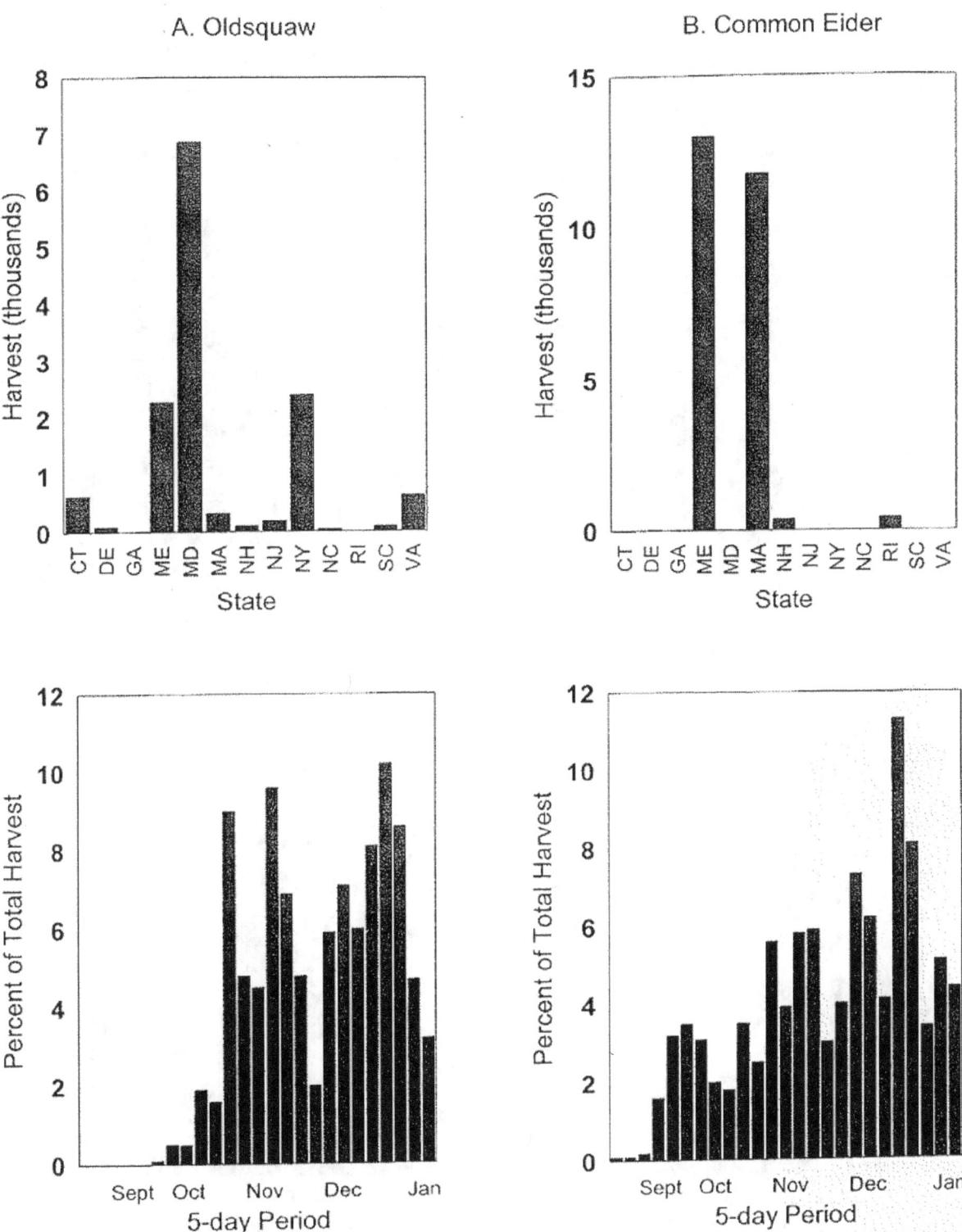

Fig. 7. Average spatial and temporal distribution of the harvest of oldsquaws (A) and common eiders (B) in states of the Atlantic Flyway, 1987-1996.

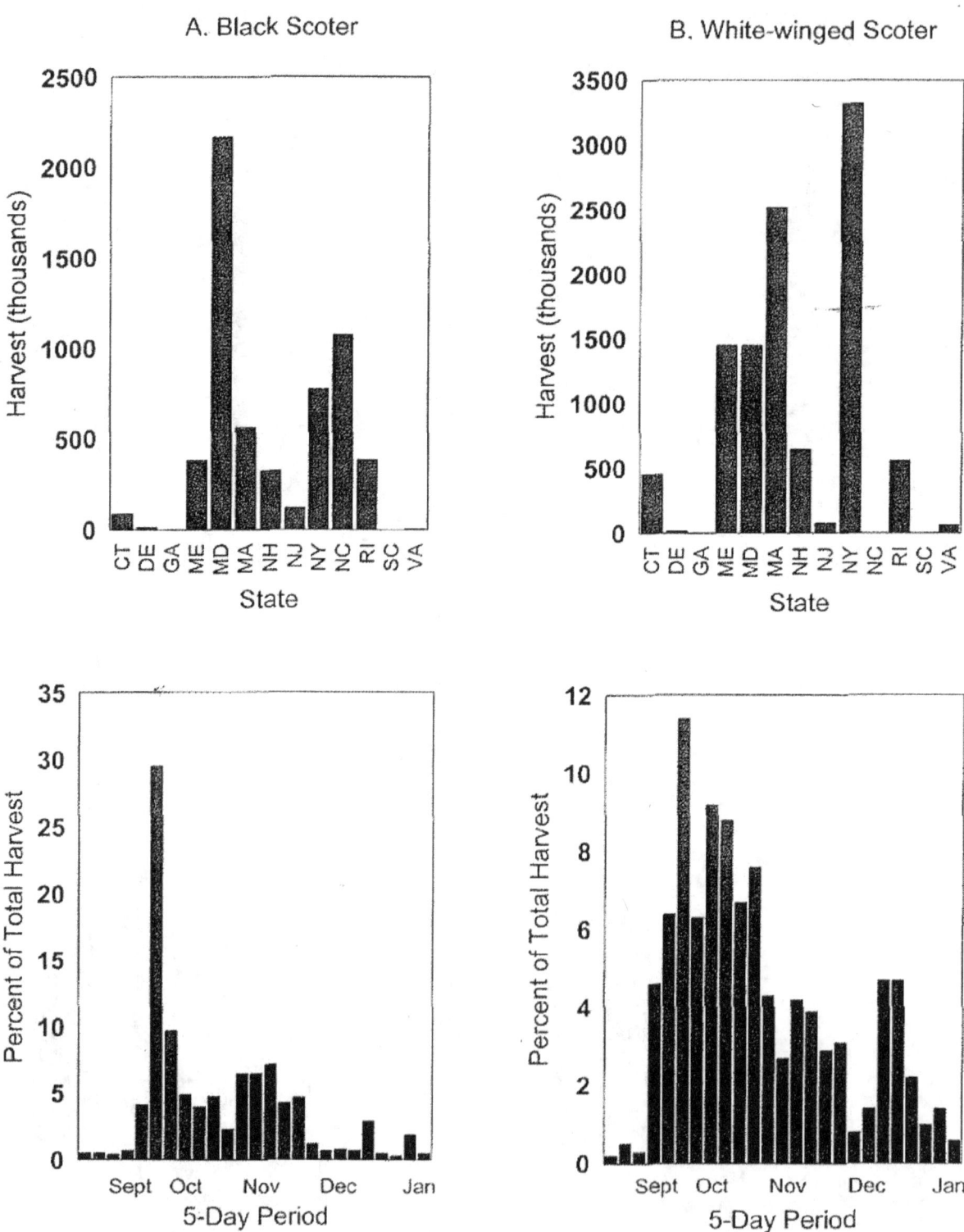

Fig. 8. Average spatial and temporal distribution of the harvest of black (A) and white-winged scoter (B) in states of the Atlantic Flyway, 1987-1996.

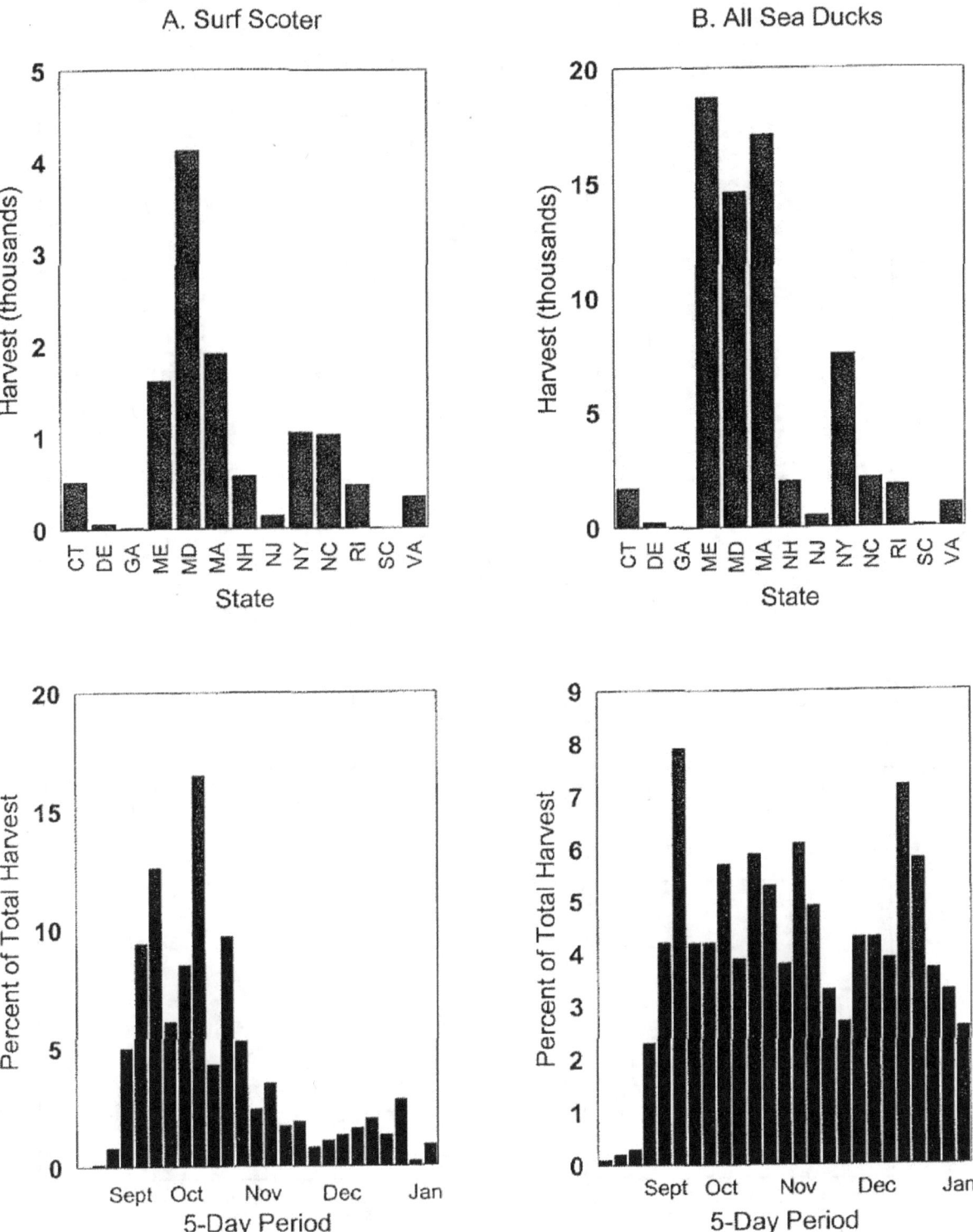

Fig. 9. Average spatial and temporal distribution of the harvest of surf scoter (A) and all sea ducks (B) in states of the Atlantic Flyway, 1987-1996.

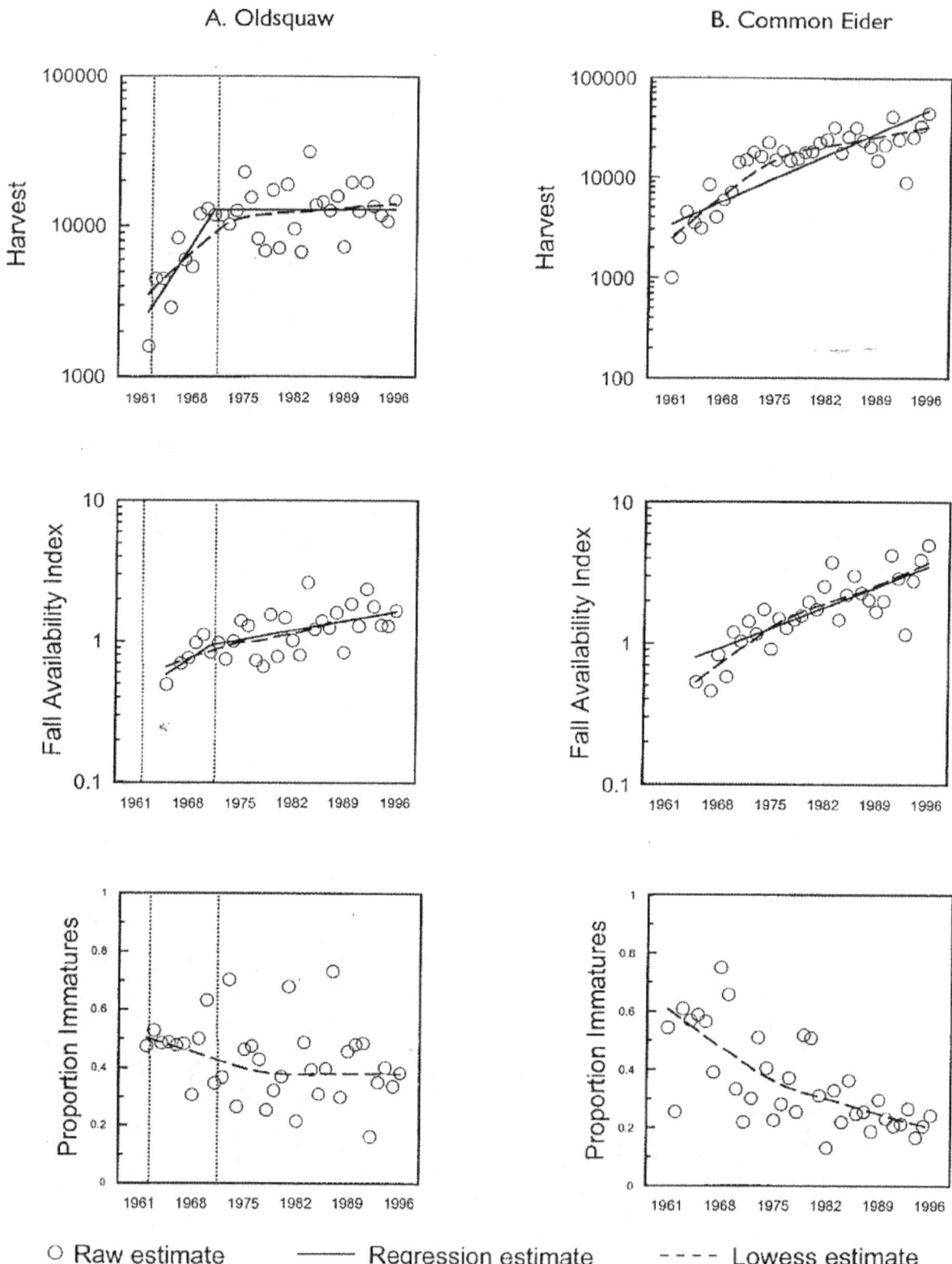

A. Oldsquaw

B. Common Eider

○ Raw estimate   ——— Regression estimate   - - - - Lowess estimate

Fig. 10. Estimates of harvest, proportion of young in the harvest, and fall availability indices for oldsquaw (A) and common eider (B) in the Atlantic Flyway, 1961-1996. Vertical lines mark periods with major differences in hunting regulations.

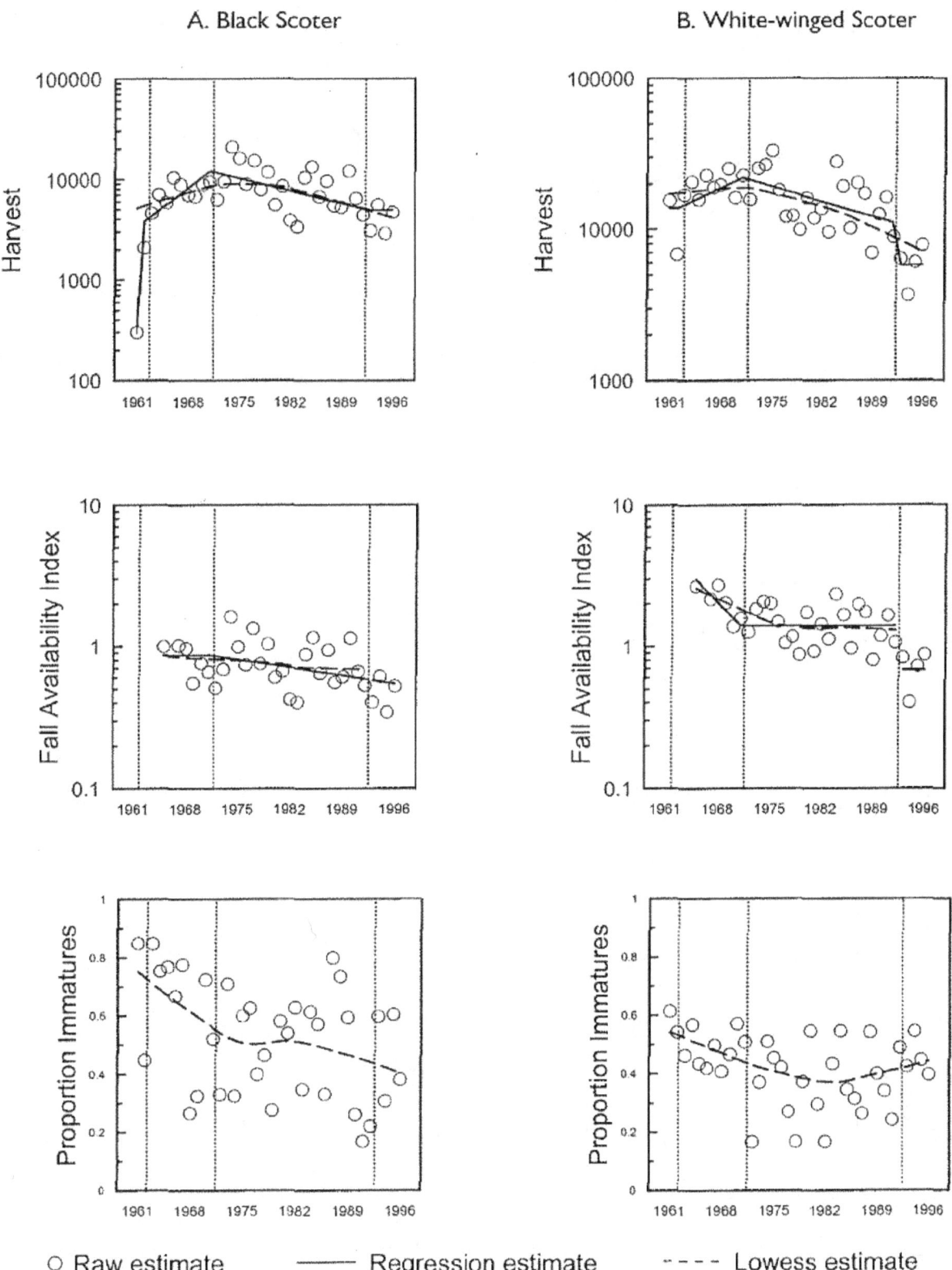

Fig. 11. Estimates of harvest, proportion of young in the harvest, and fall availability indices for black scoter (A) and white-winged scoter (B) in the Atlantic Flyway, 1961-1996. Vertical lines mark periods with major differences in hunting regulations.

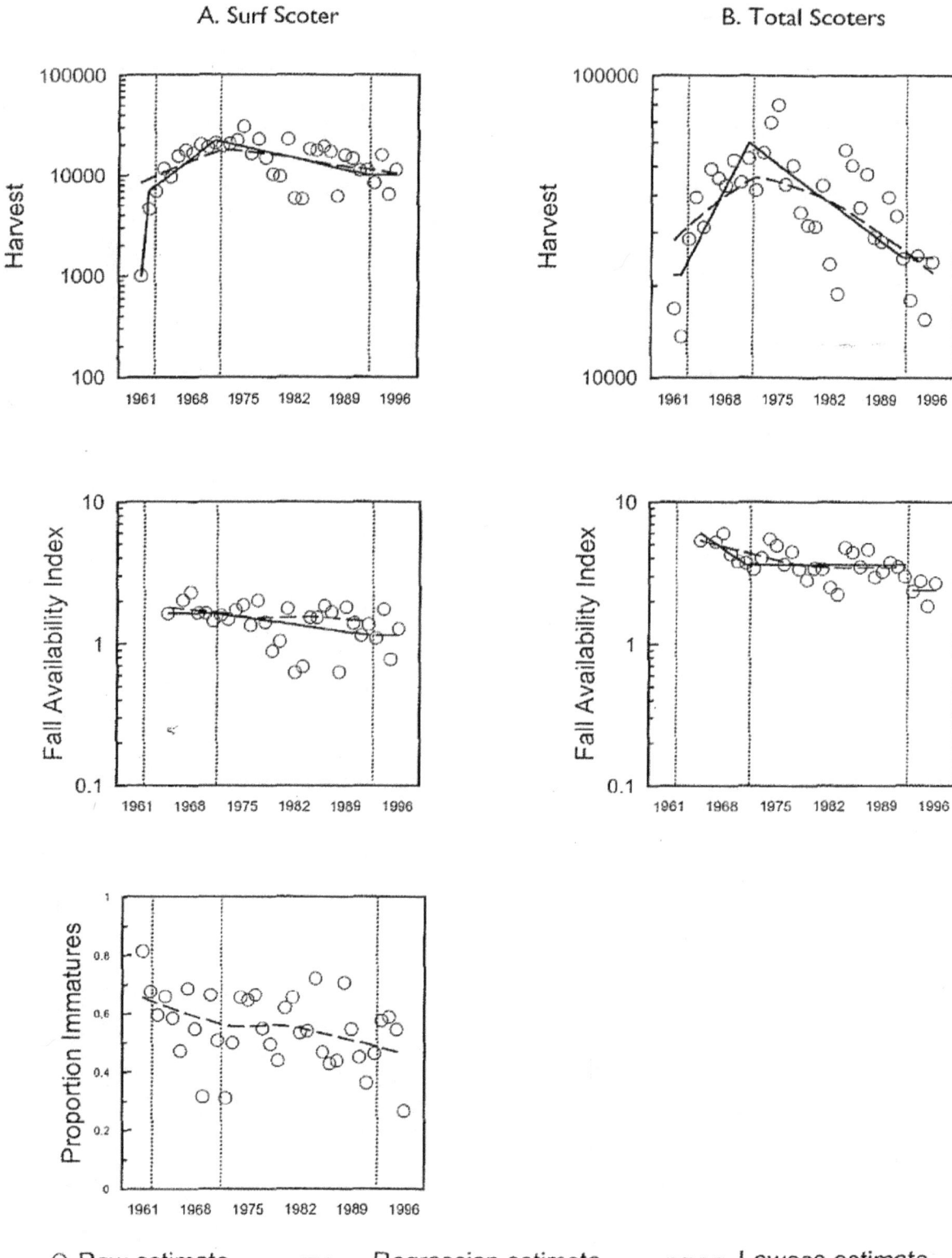

Fig. 12. Estimates of harvest, proportion of young in the harvest, and fall availability indices for surf scoter (A) and total scoters (B) in the Atlantic Flyway, 1961-1996. Vertical lines mark periods with major differences in hunting regulations.

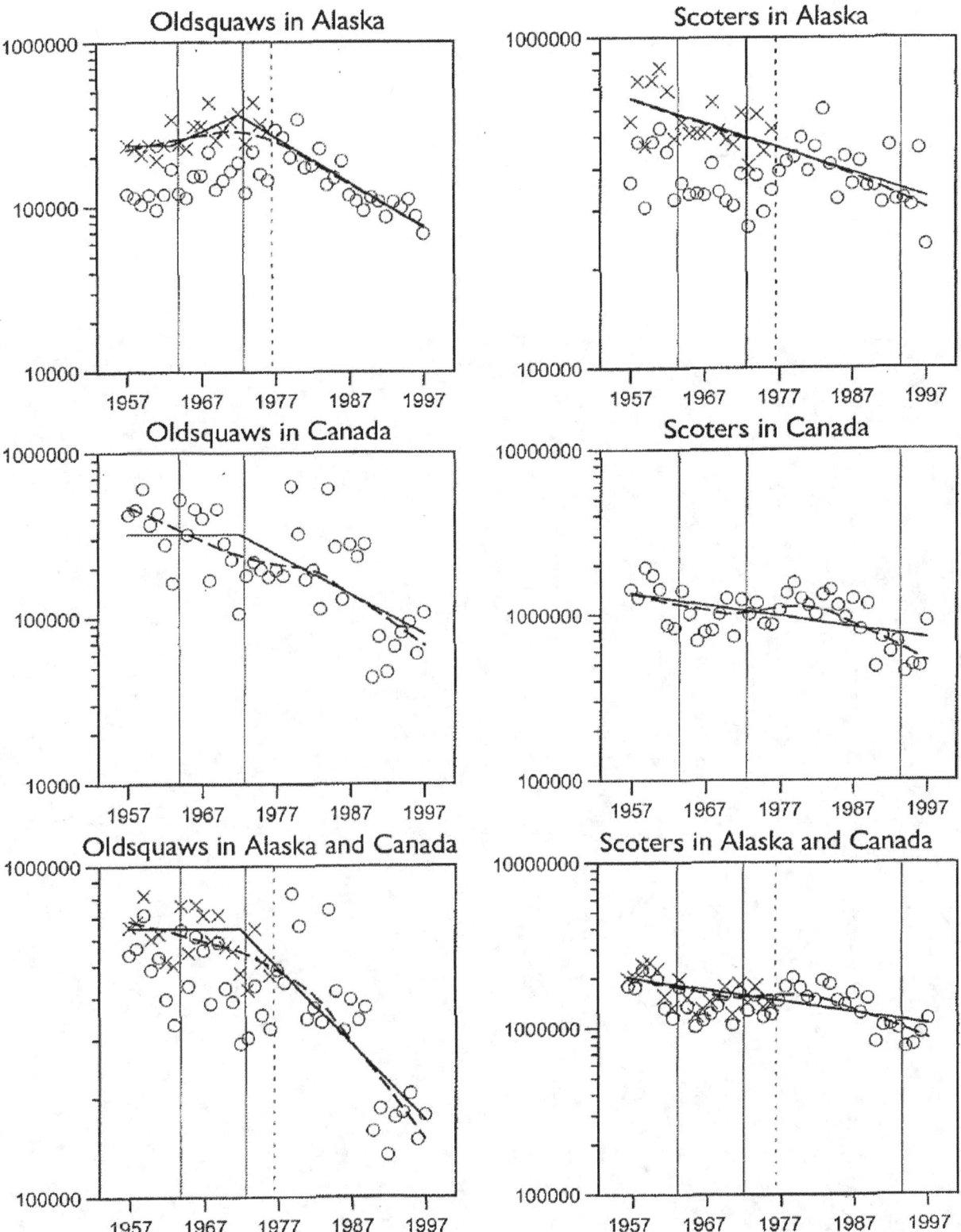

Fig. 13. Breeding population estimates of oldsquaws and scoters, 1957-1997 (X = estimate adjusted for change in aircraft type, O = unadjusted estimate, —— = regression estimate, — — = lowess estimate). Solid vertical lines mark periods with major differences in hunting regulations in the Atlantic Flyway; dashed vertical lines mark change in aircraft type.

Oldsquaw

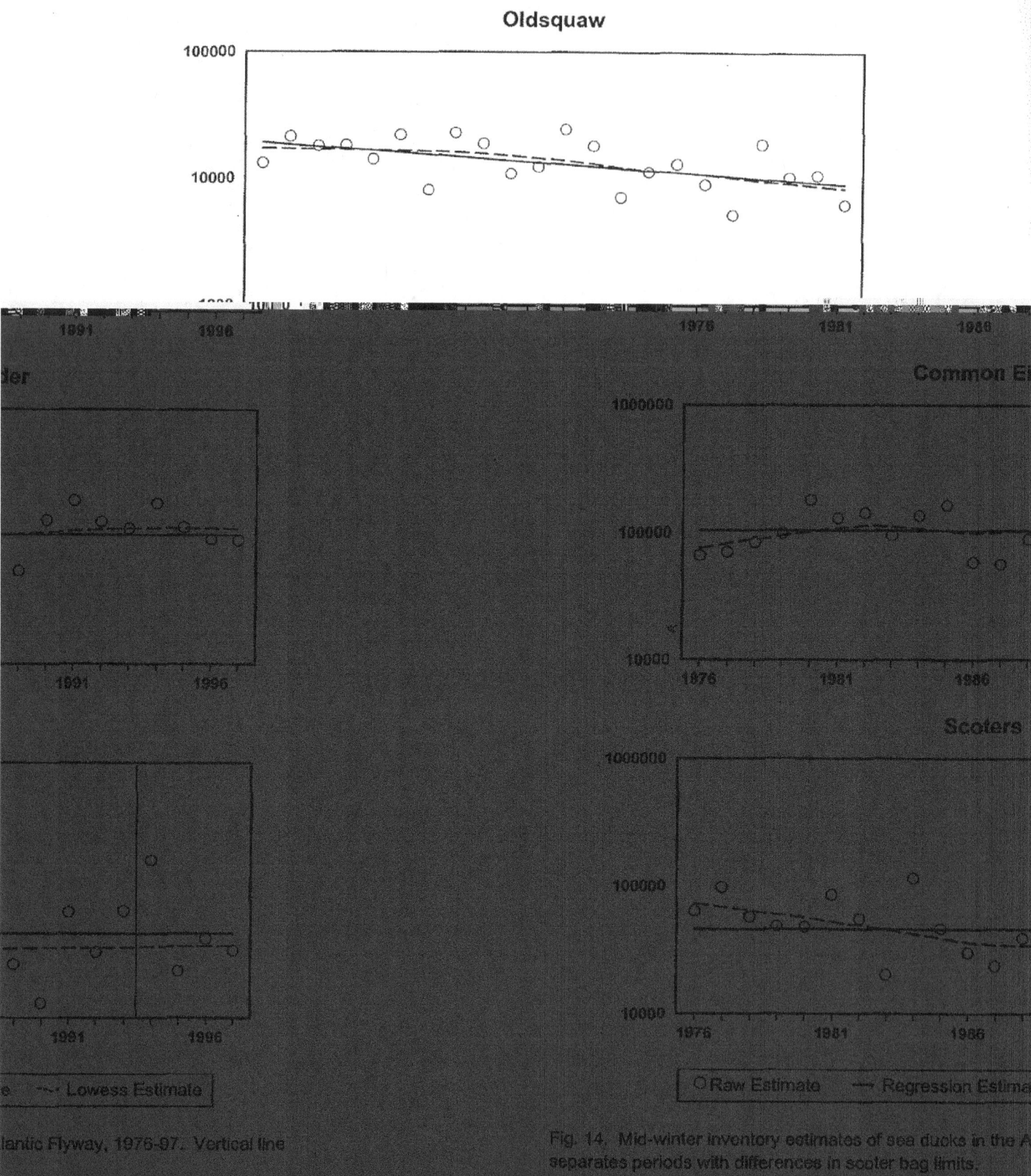

Fig. 14. Mid-winter inventory estimates of sea ducks in the Atlantic Flyway, 1976-97. Vertical line separates periods with differences in scoter bag limits.

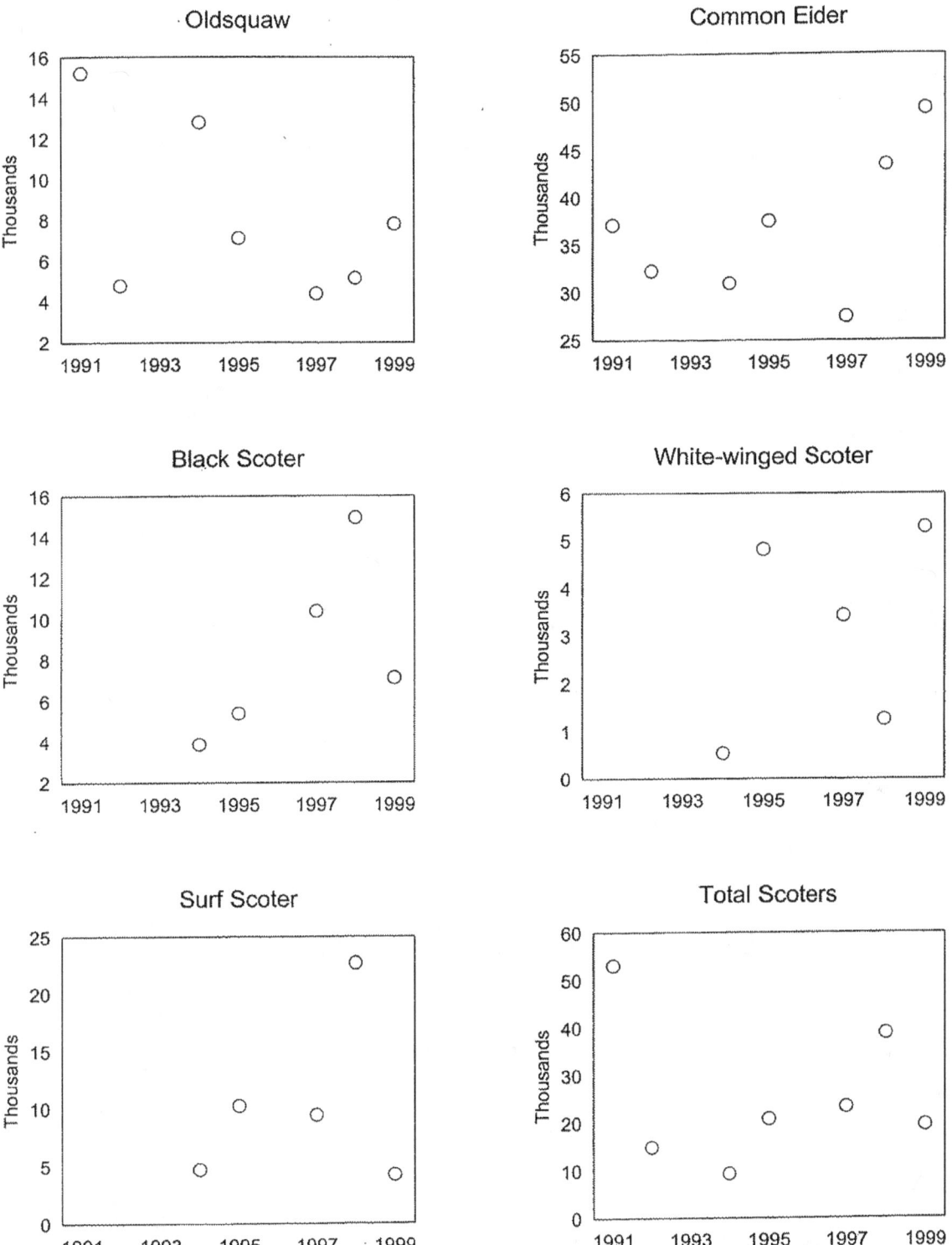

Fig. 15. Counts of sea ducks in the Sea Duck Survey of the Atlantic coast, 1991-1999. Most scoters were not identified to species in the 1991 and 1992 survey.

Appendix 1. Summary of sea duck hunting regulations in Atlantic Flyway states with special sea duck seasons (Connecticut, Delaware, Georgia, Maine, Maryland, Massachusetts, New Hampshire, New Jersey, New York, North Carolina, Rhode Island, South Carolina, and Virginia), 1938-97.

Year(s)	States(s)	Sea duck season				Eligible species	Zones	Regular season		Total sea duck days
		Opening date	Closing date	Days	Bag			Days	Bag	
1938-39	ME, NH	9/15	9/30	16	10	Scoters	Beyond outer harbor lines[1]	45	10	61
	CT, MA, RI,	9/15	10/14	30	10	"	"	45	10	75
	Others							45	10	45
1940-41	ME, NH	9/15	9/30	16	10	"	"	60	10	76
	CT, MA, NY, RI	9/15	10/15	31	10	"	"	60	10	91
	Others							60	10	60
1942-43	ME, NH	9/15	9/24-25	10-11	10	"	"	70	10	80-81
	CT, MA, NY, RI	9/15	10/14	30	10	"	"	70	10	100
	Others							70	10	70
1944-45	ME, NH	9/15	9/19	5	10	"	"	80	10	85
	CT, MA, NY, RI	9/15	9/30-10/12	16-28	10	"	"	80	10	96-108
	Others							80	10	80
1946	ME, NH	9/15	10/4	20	7	"	"	45	7	65
	CT, MA, NY, RI	9/15	10/25	41	7	"	"	45	7	86
	Others							45	7	45
1947	ME	10/6	12/16	72	7	"	"	24	4	72
	NH	9/1	10/6	36	7	"	"	24	4	66
	NY	9/16	12/13	89	7	"	"	24	4	89
	CT, MA	9/16	11/17	63	7	"	"	30	4	93
	RI	9/16	12/1	77	7	"	"	30	4	107
	Others							24-30	4	24-30
1948	MA, NY, CT, RI	9/18	12/17	91	7	Scoters, eiders	"	24-30	4	91
	ME	10/6	12/16	72	7	"	"	24	4	72
	NH	9/1	10/7	37	7	"	"	24	4	61
	Others							24-30	4	24-30
1949	New England[2], NY	9/17	12/17	92	7	"	"	32-40	4	92
	Others							32-40	4	32-40
1950	New England[2], NY	9/17	12/17	92	7	Scoters, eiders, oldsquaw		32-40	4	92
	Others							32-40	4	32-40
1951	CT, ME, MA, NH, NY	9/28	12/31	95	7	"	"	36-45	4	36-45
	RI	9/28	1/5	100	7	"	"	45	4	45
	Others							45	4	45

Appendix 1. Continued

Year(s)	States(s)	Sea duck season Opening date	Closing date	Days	Bag	Eligible species	Zones	Regular season Days	Bag	Total sea duck days
1952	ME, MA, NH, NY	9/28	12/31	95	7	Scoters, eiders, oldsquaw	Beyond outer harbor lines[1]	44-55	4	95
	CT	10/17	12/31	76	7	"	"	55	4	76
	RI	9/28	1/5	100	7	"	"	55	4	100
	Others							55	4	55
1953-54	ME, MA, NH, RI	9/16	12/31	107	7	"	"	54-60	4	107
	CT, NY	10/1	12/31	92	7	"	"	60	4	92
	Others							42-60	4	42-60
1955-57	ME, MA, NH, RI	9/14-16	12/29-31	107	7	"	"	70	4	107
	CT, NY	10/1	12/31	92	7	"	"	70	4	92
	Others							70	4	70
1958	New England[2], NY	10/1	1/15	107	7	"	"	54-60	4	107
	Others							60	4	60
1959-60	New England[2], NY	10/1	1/8	100	7	"	"	45-50	3	100
	Others							40-50	3-4	40-50
1961-62	New England[2], NY	10/1	1/8	100	7	"	"	36-50	2-3	100
	Others							40-50	2-3	40-50
1963	New England[2], NY	10/1	1/15	107	7	"	Upstream to first bridge[3]	45-59	2	107
	Others							40-50	2-4	40-50
1964-65	New England[2], NY	9/25	1/10	108	7	"	"	45-50	3	108
	Others							40-50	3-4	40-50
1966	New England[2], NY	9/25	1/10	108	7	"	"	50-55	3	108
	MD, NJ, NC	9/25	1/10	108	7	"	≥1 mile from shore[4]	50-55	3	108
	Others							45-55	3-4	45-55
1967	New England[2], NY	9/25	1/10	108	7	"	[3]	45-50	3	108
	MD, NJ, NC	9/25	1/10	108	7	"	[4]	50	3	108
	Others							40-50	3-4	40-50
1968	New England[2], NY	9/25	1/10	108	7	"	[3]	45-50	3	108
	GA, MD, NJ, NC, SC, VA	9/25	1/10	108	7	"	[4]	40-50	3-4	108
	DE							50	3	50
1969	New England[2], NY	9/25	1/10	108	7	"	[3]	45-57	3	108
	GA, NJ, NC, SC, VA	9/25	1/10	108	7	"	[4]	40-57	3-4	108
	MD	9/25	1/10	108	7	"	≥1200 yards from shore[5]	50	3	108
	DE							50	3	50

Appendix 1. Continued

Year(s)	States(s)	Sea duck season						Regular season		Total sea duck days
		Opening date	Closing date	Days	Bag	Eligible species	Zones	Days	Bag	
1970	New England[2], NY	9/25	1/10	108	7	Scoters, eiders, oldsquaw	3	50-60	3-4	108
	GA, NC, SC, VA	9/25	1/10	108	7	"	4	50-60	3-4	108
	NJ	9/25	1/10	108	7	"	4	60	Point system	108
	MD	9/25	1/10	108	7	"	≥ 800 yards from shore[6]	50	4	108
	DE							50	4	50
1971	New England[2], NY	9/25	1/9	107	7	"	3	50-60	3-4	107
	DE, GA, NC, SC	9/25	1/9	107	7	"	4	50-60	3-4	107
	MD, VA	9/25	1/9	107	7	"	6	60	3	107
	NJ	9/25	1/9	107	7	"	4	60	Point system	107
1972	New England[2], NY	9/23	1/7	107	7	"	3	45-60	3-4	107
	GA, NC, SC	9/23	1/7	107	7	"	4	50	4-5	107
	DE, MD, VA	9/23	1/7	107	7	"	6	50-60	3-4	107
	NJ	9/23	1/7	107	7	"	4	60	Point system	107
1973[7]	New England[2], NY	9/15-29	12/30-1/12	107	7	"	3	40-45	4	107
	DE, MD, NC, SC	9/29-10/5	1/13-19	107	7	"	4(NC, SC), 6(DE, MD)	45	5	107
	NJ, VA	9/1-21	12/16-1/5	107	7		4(NJ), 6(VA)	50	Point system	107
	GA	Closed	Closed					45	5	45
1974[7]	CT, ME, MA, NH, NY	9/20-28	1/4-11	107	7	"	3	50	4	107
	DE, SC	9/20-10/4	1/4-18	107	7	"	4(SC), 6(DE)	50	5	107
	MD, NJ, NC, RI, VA	9/25-10/6	1/9-20	107	7		3(RI), 4(NJ, NC), 6(MD, VA)	55	Point system	107
	GA	Closed	Closed					50	5	50
1975[7]	CT, ME, MA, NH	9/15-10/15	12/30-1/20	107	7	"	3	50	4	107
	DE, NY, SC	9/20-10/6	1/8-20	107	7		3(NY), 4(SC), 6(DE)	50	5	107
	MD, NJ, NC, RI, VA	9/19-10/4	1/3-17	107	7		3(RI), 4(NJ), 6(MD, NC, VA)	50	5	107
	GA	11/19	1/20	63	7			50	5	63
1976-80[8,9]	MD, NJ, RI,VA	9/18-10/6	1/1-20	107	7	"	3,4,6	50	Point system	107
	GA	11/16-27	1/20	55-66	7	"	4	50	5	55-66
	Others	9/15-10/15	12/30-1/20	107	7	"	3,4,6	50	4-5	107
1981-84[8,9]	MD, NJ, VA	10/5-6	1/19-20	107	7	"	4,6	50	Point system	107
	GA	11/22-25	1/20	57-59	7	"	4	50	5	57-59
	Others	9/15-10/6	12/30-1/20	107	7	"	3,4,6	50	4-5	107
1985-87[8,9]	GA	11/26-29	1/12-18	45-53	7	"	4	50	4-5	107
	Others	9/15-10/6	12/30-1/20	107	7	"	3,4,6	40	4	45-53
1988[8,9]	GA	11/24	1/8	46	7	"	4	30	4	46
	Others	9/15-10/6	12/30-1/20	107	7	"	3,4,6	30	3	107

Appendix 1. Continued

Year(s)	States(s)	Sea duck season						Regular season		Total sea duck days
		Opening date	Closing date	Days	Bag	Eligible species	Zones	Days	Bag	
1989-92[8,9]	GA	11/22-28	1/5-10	39-46	7	Scoters, eiders, oldsquaw	4	30	3	39-46
	MD	10/9-13	1/19-20	100-104	5	"	6	30	3	100-104
	Others	9/15-10/6	12/30-1/20	107	7	"	3, 4, 6	30	3	107
1993[8,9]	GA	11/25	1/16	53	7 (4 scoters)	"	4	30	3	53
	MD	10/8	1/20	105	5 (4 scoters)	"	6	30	3	105
	Others	9/15-10/6	12/30-1/20	107	7 (4 scoters)	"	3, 4, 6	30	3	107
1994[8,9]	GA	11/23	1/20	59	7 (4 scoters)	"	4	40	3	59
	MD	10/6	1/20	107	5 (4 scoters)	"	6	40	3	107
	Others	9/15-10/6	12/30-1/20	107	7 (4 scoters)	"	3,4,6	40	3	107
1995-96[8,9]	GA	11/22-27	1/20	55-60	7 (4 scoters)	"	4	50	5	55-60
	MD	10/6-7	1/20	106-107	5 (4 scoters)	"	6	50	4	106-107
	Others	9/15-10/11	12/30-1/20	107	7 (4 scoters)	"	3,4,6	50	3-5	107
1997[8,9]	GA	11/22	1/20	60	7 (4 scoters)	"	4	60	6	60
	MD	10/6	1/20	107	5 (4 scoters)	"	6	60	4	107
	Others	9/15-10/10	12/30-1/20	107[10]	7 (4 scoters)	"	3,4,6	60	4-6	107

[1] In coastal waters only, beyond outer harbor lines.
[2] CT, ME, MA, NH, RI.
[3] All coastal waters and all waters of rivers and streams lying seaward from the first upstream bridge.
[4] Any waters of the Atlantic Ocean, and/or any tidal waters of any bay, that are separated by ≥ 1 mile of open water from any shore, island, or emergent vegetation.
[5] Any waters of the Atlantic Ocean, and/or any tidal waters of any bay, that are separated by ≥ 1200 yards of open water from any shore, island, or emergent vegetation.
[6] Any waters of the Atlantic Ocean, and/or any tidal waters of any bay, that are separated by ≥ 800 yards of open water from any shore, island, or emergent vegetation.
[7] States were allowed to select a sea duck season of up to 107 consecutive days during the period 9/1-1/20, inclusive.
[8] States were allowed to select a sea duck season of up to 107 consecutive days, during the periods 9/18-1/20 (1976-77), 9/16-1/20 (1978), or 9/15-1/20 (1979-97).
[9] No substantive changes have been made to special sea duck zones since 1975.
[10] Includes compensatory days for states in which Sunday hunting is prohibited.

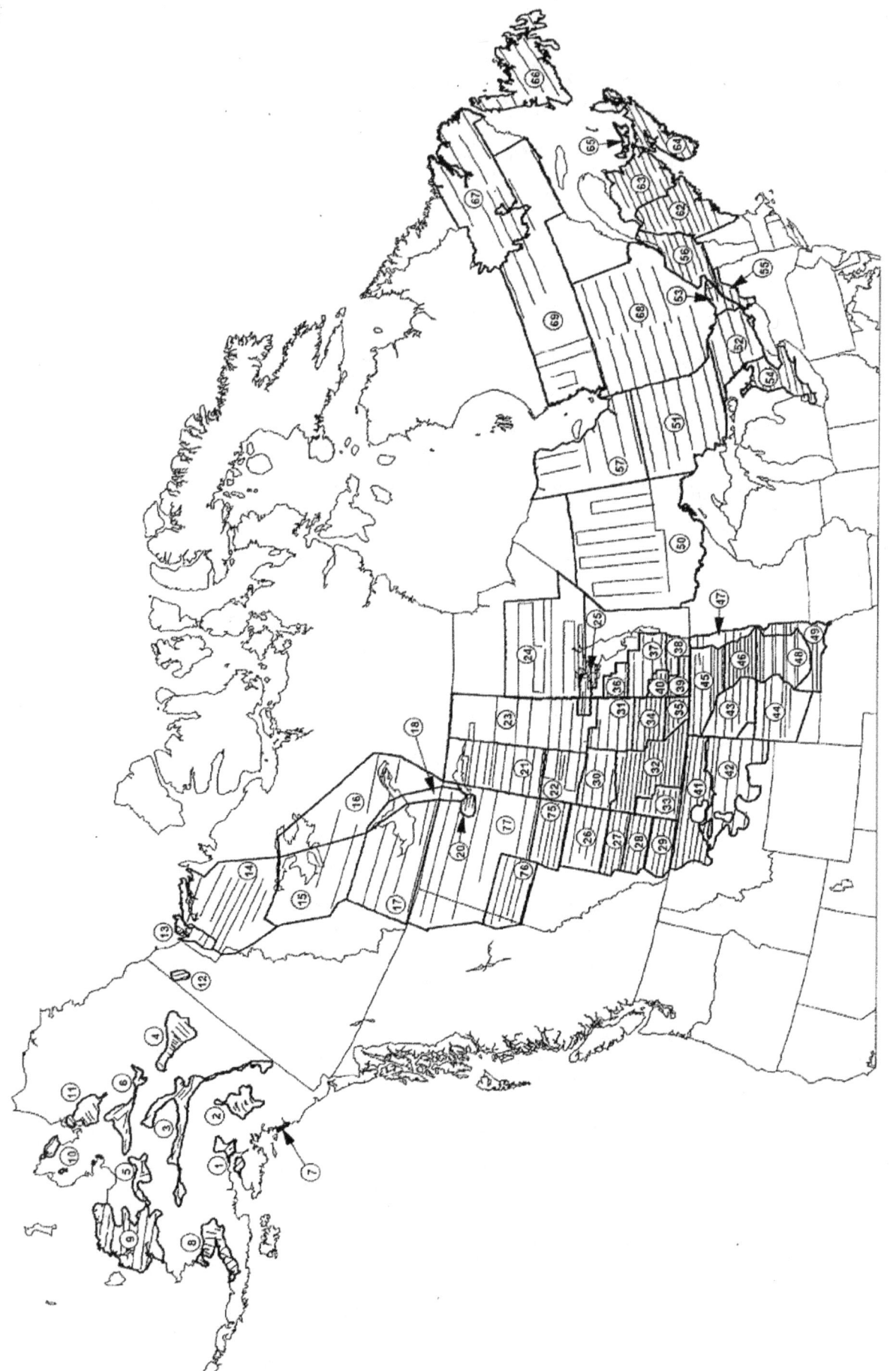

Appendix 2. Transects and strata of the Breeding Waterfowl and Habitat Survey. Some strata were not surveyed in all years.

Appendix 3. Autoregressive Moving Average (ARMA) time series models.

We report on these parts of the models separately since the time series errors are asymptotically independent from the regression. The series are short, so we could only fit simple time series models to the regression residuals. Most series showed no time series error structure; simple one parameter first order autoregressive or moving average structure could explain those exhibiting error structure. The following table shows the ARMA structure where ϕ_1 is the first order autoregressive parameter, and θ_1 is the first order moving average parameter. The variance column shows the residual or innovation variance; $i.e.$, the variance after the regression after accounted for the time series error structure. The variance and AIC are not comparable between series, $e.g.$, between oldsquaw and common eider harvests. They are listed for reference purposes.

In the table below, "AIC" is a statistic describing each chosen model. Lower AIC values indicate better model performance. "AIC difference" (AIC of chosen model minus AIC of alternative model) represents the results of a comparison of models with and without an ARMA time series error structure. Negative differences indicate that the chosen model performed better than the alternative model. Differences ≥ 2 are significant, so differences greater than +2 would indicate choosing a significantly worse model. In some cases, a model with a higher AIC was chosen, but the difference was never >2. In other cases the autocorrelations did not indicate that the residuals were anything but independent. In these cases, no test was done, and we relied on the Autocorrelation Function (ACF) in place of the test.

Series	ARMA Model	Variance	AIC	AIC Difference
Harvest				
Oldsquaw	$\theta_1=0.52$	0.12	678.8	-2.0
Common Eider	$\theta_1=0.62$	0.18	734.7	ACF
Black Scoter	None	0.16	679.2	ACF
White-Winged Scoter	None	0.12	723.9	ACF
Surf Scoter	None	0.13	719.3	ACF
All Scoters	None	0.09	776.7	0.2
Availability Index				
Oldsquaw	None	0.12	30.3	0.3
Eider	None	0.14	66.0	ACF
Black Scoter	None	0.11	8.4	ACF
White-Winged Scoter	None	0.10	47.8	ACF
Surf Scoter	None	0.10	45.7	ACF
All Scoters	None	0.04	82.8	ACF
Breeding Waterfowl Survey				
Alaska Oldsquaw	None	0.03	958.9	-1.8
US+Canada Oldsquaw	None	0.28	1074.2	ACF
North America Oldsquaw	None	0.07	1074.8	0.7
Alaska Scoters	$\phi_1=-0.35$	0.02	1026.7	-2.2
US+Canada Scoters	None	0.07	1151.6	ACF
North America Scoters	$\phi_1=0.45$	0.03	1151.2	-6.8
Mid-winter Inventory				
Oldsquaw	None	0.13	442.9	ACF
Common Eider	None	0.14	533.4	0.7
All Scoters	None	0.36	516.7	ACF

Appendix 4. Estimated total harvest of sea ducks in eastern Canada[1] and the Atlantic Flyway of the U.S., and the percent of the harvest occurring in each area, 1974-1997.

Year	Oldsquaw			Harlequin duck			Common eider			King eider		
	Harvest	% Canada	%U.S.	Harvest	% Canada	%U.S.	Harvest	% Canada	%U.S.	Harvest	% Canada	%U.S.
1974	25,500	50	50	100	100	0	33,200	33	67	100	100	0
1975	44,000	48	52	0			36,700	60	40	0		
1976	36,000	57	43	0			54,500	67	33	0		
1977	17,000	51	49	100	0	100	52,400	72	28	200	100	0
1978	17,100	60	40	0			48,100	68	32	500	20	80
1979	37,000	53	47	200	100	0	40,300	56	44	400	100	0
1980	24,700	71	29	200	0	100	45,900	61	39	0		
1981	33,200	44	56	0			47,200	53	47	400	100	0
1982	27,200	65	35	0			46,700	49	51	900	100	0
1983	26,500	75	25	0			81,800	61	39	0		
1984	60,000	48	52	500	100	0	51,500	66	34	0		
1985	25,400	45	55	0			45,100	44	56	300	100	0
1986	30,500	52	48	1,900	100	0	61,500	48	52	1,600	94	6
1987	24,000	47	53	1,300	100	0	48,600	52	48	1,300	100	0
1988	26,400	41	59	1,200	100	0	42,000	52	48	100	100	0
1989	16,500	56	44	300	100	0	38,200	62	38	200	100	0
1990	25,400	24	76	200	100	0	47,600	56	44	600	100	0
1991	17,500	29	71	200	100	0	63,900	36	64	500	80	20
1992	25,900	25	75	0			61,500	61	39	600	100	0
1993	19,600	31	69	100	100	0	33,300	73	27	1,000	100	0
1994	19,100	38	62	300	100	0	43,100	42	58	100	100	0
1995	16,700	36	64	400	100	0	54,300	40	60	700	100	0
1996	24,800	40	60	0			63,500	30	70	300	100	0
1997	21,700	25	75	0			55,200	36	64	200	0	100
Min	16,500	24	25	0	0	0	33,200	30	27	0	0	0
Max	60,000	75	76	1,900	100	100	81,800	73	70	1,600	100	100
Mean	26,738	46	54	292	86	14	49,838	53	47	417	89	11

Appendix 4. Continued.

Year	Black scoter			White-winged scoter			Surf scoter			Total sea ducks		
	Harvest	% Canada	%U.S.	Harvest	% Canada	%U.S.	Harvest	% Canada	%U.S.	Harvest	% Canada	%U.S.
1974	33,700	38	62	42,200	37	63	38,800	43	57	173,600	40	60
1975	41,800	61	39	44,200	25	75	58,300	48	52	225,000	48	52
1976	41,300	78	22	33,000	45	55	58,800	72	28	223,600	65	35
1977	52,400	71	29	27,500	56	44	56,000	59	41	205,600	64	36
1978	18,000	56	44	23,000	47	53	31,100	52	48	137,800	58	42
1979	28,400	58	42	25,000	60	40	33,200	70	30	164,500	59	41
1980	20,900	73	27	37,200	57	43	31,600	69	31	160,500	65	35
1981	31,700	73	27	24,300	51	49	44,900	49	51	181,700	54	46
1982	20,500	80	20	25,900	47	53	35,200	83	17	156,400	63	37
1983	14,600	77	23	22,200	57	43	16,600	65	35	161,700	65	35
1984	23,900	56	44	46,600	40	60	36,500	50	50	219,000	52	48
1985	26,100	49	51	31,900	39	61	29,800	41	59	158,600	44	56
1986	15,600	56	44	14,700	31	69	28,500	32	68	154,300	46	54
1987	20,400	52	48	32,200	37	63	31,000	45	55	158,800	48	52
1988	11,300	51	49	30,000	42	58	17,800	65	35	128,800	50	50
1989	12,100	56	44	18,800	63	37	30,600	48	52	116,700	57	43
1990	19,100	37	63	22,000	43	57	32,600	55	45	147,500	46	54
1991	13,900	53	47	20,500	20	80	17,900	37	63	134,400	35	65
1992	8,800	50	50	16,200	45	55	17,400	35	65	130,400	48	52
1993	10,100	69	31	14,300	55	45	19,600	57	43	98,000	59	41
1994	11,900	53	47	13,200	72	28	34,500	54	46	122,200	49	51
1995	7,800	63	37	10,400	41	59	19,100	66	34	109,400	46	54
1996	8,300	43	57	12,700	38	62	16,900	33	67	126,500	34	66
1997	8,400	45	55	10,900	37	63	16,400	41	59	112,800	35	65
Min	7,800	37	20	10,400	20	28	16,400	32	17	98,000	34	35
Max	52,400	80	63	46,600	72	80	58,800	83	68	225,000	65	66
Mean	20,875	58	42	24,954	45	55	31,379	53	47	154,492	51	49

[1]Includes New Brunswick, Newfoundland, Nova Scotia, Prince Edward Island, and Quebec.